How to thrive in a shattered world

HOPE
FOR TROUBLED TIMES

MARK FINLEY

Stanborough Press Ltd.
Established since 1884 | www.stanboroughpress.org.uk

This book was
Edited by: James Cavil
Copyedited by: Rhonda Christiano
Desktop layout by: Melinda Worden
Cover designed by: Peter Oppong-Mensah

PRINTED IN THAILAND.

ISBN 978-1-78665-131-0

To order,
call +44(0)1476 591700 or email sales@stanboroughpress.org.uk

Visit www.stanboroughpress.org.uk for information on other
Stanborough Press products.

CONTENTS

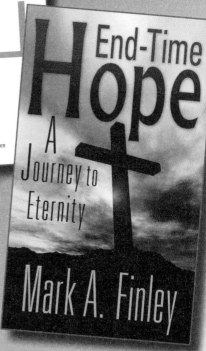

PREFACE
HOPE FOR TROUBLED TIMES

A Personal Word From Mark Finley

Recently our world has gone through a devastating pandemic. Although some countries were hit much harder than others, the entire world has been impacted. Millions have been infected. Hundreds of thousands have died. The global economy has been severely disrupted, and we are just beginning to recover. In a sense COVID-19 has touched us all, but the coronavirus is not the only tragedy that our world is facing in the twenty-first century. There are a number of significant challenges we are facing personally and as a global community.

Unemployment, poverty, natural disasters, cancer, heart disease, rising crime, increased violence, war, and famine are affecting millions. These world conditions lead us to ask a series of questions: Where is God in all of this? Is God responsible for the catastrophes in our world? Are we living at the time of the end? Are these climactic events predicted in prophecy? How can we live purposeful, joyous lives in the light of everything going on in our world? The Bible provides answers to these and many other questions. In this book, *Hope for Troubled Times*, we will explore God's answers to our deepest questions.

The book you hold in your hands is all about hope—hope for today, tomorrow, and forever. You will find answers here that satisfy your mind and fill your heart with peace and joy. I have written this book with you in mind. Every page will encourage you on life's journey, so come with me on a journey to the very heart of God and discover a God who loves you more than you can ever imagine, and has a plan for this world that is amazing. You will thrill at how good God is, and you will find a new sense of security and hope. So read on and discover God's plan for our planet.

Mark Finley

CHAPTER 1

PANDEMICS, PESTILENCES, AND PROPHECY

Our world has experienced a crisis of pandemic proportions. A fast-moving virus has ravaged country after country at lightning speed. The coronavirus has changed life as we knew it. COVID-19 is a strain of the virus family that we haven't seen before. Presently researchers are in a race against time to develop scientifically tested and approved vaccines for this rapidly spreading virus. During the height of the virus international borders were closed. Schools suspended classes. Businesses mandated their workers to work from home. Restaurants closed. Movie theaters, amusement parks, and other entertainment venues shut their doors. Sporting events and large conventions were canceled. People were told to avoid gatherings of more than 10 individuals. "Social distancing" became a common theme in the news media. Federal and state agencies placed entire cities on lockdown. In some countries the medical system became overwhelmed. The international stock market plunged. Unemployment rates skyrocketed.

Reports of the coronavirus dominated the news for months. International and local media outlets gave it round-the-clock coverage. The front pages of newspapers featured it daily. We had daily briefings and updates from public health officials. The entire world seemed to be consumed with this tiny, easily transmittable virus. At times we were left with more questions than answers. Many of those questions revolved around religious themes. Deep within our hearts we were seeking answers.

Answering the Tough Questions

Where is God in all this? Is COVID-19 a judgment of God, or is it just some random, out-of-control virus? What does the Bible say about pestilences or pandemics? Is this a sign of the end of the world?

Hope for Troubled Times

Is there hope on the horizon—hope for our personal lives, our families, our children, and our world? Let me assure you, God is not the author of sickness. He is not the originator of suffering or disease. In the first chapter of the Bible, at the end of Creation week, God looked out over the world and declared that "it was very good" (Genesis 1:31). God created a perfect world without one taint of disease. There were no viruses, germs, or bacteria. There was no suffering or death. Sickness was not part of His original plan. His plan was for earth to be populated with people who were happy, healthy, and holy.

Sin is an intruder that entered our world through an angelic being called Lucifer. This being of dazzling brightness, created perfect by God, rebelled against the principles of God's government in heaven millenniums ago. This fallen angel is behind all the suffering in our world. God created each of His creatures with the freedom of choice. To take away the freedom of choice is to remove the capacity to love. Without love, life has little meaning. Without love, genuine happiness is not possible. Lucifer chose the way of selfishness rather than the way of love.

This same fallen angel deceived Adam and Eve, just as he deceived one third of the angels in heaven. The Bible calls the devil "a liar and the father of lies" (John 8:44, NIV). The Bible's last book, Revelation, describes him as the one who "deceives the whole world" (Revelation 12:9). Satan's first lie was that God did not mean what He said. Eve could partake of the tree of the knowledge of good and evil and would not "surely die," as God had declared (Genesis 3:4). She could violate God's commands without any serious consequences. The evil one deceived her into thinking that by eating of the tree she would enter a higher sphere of existence. Satan claimed that God was arbitrary, an authoritarian tyrant who did not have the best interest of His creatures in view.

Opening a Door God Wanted Forever Shut

When Adam and Eve sinned, they opened a door of sickness, suffering, and disease that God wanted forever shut. Sin is essentially separation from God (see Isaiah 59:1, 2). Separated from God, we are separated from the ultimate source of life. Separated from God, we are

8

separated from the source of health. We live in a broken world—a world in rebellion against God. The reason Christ came was to satisfy the claims of the broken law, to restore us back to God's image, and to reveal what God is like. The Bible says in Luke 19:10 that "the Son of Man came to seek and to save the lost" (NIV). Because "the wages of sin is death," and "all have sinned, and come short of the glory of God," Christ came to redeem this lost world (Romans 6:23, 3:23, KJV). In His life and death, Jesus revealed how much the Father cares for us. Every miracle in the New Testament that Jesus performed speaks to us of a God who cares when we suffer. Every time He opened blind eyes, unstopped deaf ears, healed withered arms, and raised dead bodies to life, He demonstrated how much He genuinely loves us. By His death on the cross, He demolished Satan's lie forever and revealed that He would rather take the guilt, shame, and condemnation of sin upon Himself than have one of us lost (see 2 Corinthians 5:21, Galatians 3:13). But Jesus came also to be an example, to model the abundant life. Jesus demonstrated that God is not the one behind sickness; He's not the one behind suffering; He is not the one behind disease. He is the God of the abundant life! In the great controversy between good and evil, a rebel angel has rebelled against God and is battling against God for the control of this planet. Sickness, suffering, heartache, and disease are the result of this controversy. Satan uses sickness, suffering, and disease to discredit God. He deceives millions into thinking God does not have our best interest in view. In this world of suffering, God has revealed His love and care. He says, "*Lo, I am with you always, even unto the end of the world*" (Matthew 28:20, KJV).

What About Pestilences in the Bible?

The Bible uses the word "pestilence," or a variation of that word, 81 different times in the New King James Version. A pestilence is a sudden or fatal epidemic that generally impacts an entire community. The word "pestilence" is used at least three different ways in Scripture. Sometimes in the Bible the word "pestilence" is used to describe a disease that occurs because we are in a world of sin. Take, for example, the story of Job. Did Job's sin cause the pestilences that afflicted his body from head to toe? Was he responsible for the impact of the destruction upon his livestock, his family, his home, and his community? Certainly not! Satan was the mastermind behind all his suffering and disease. Speaking of Job's experience, the scripture states, "So Satan went out from the presence of the Lord, and struck Job with painful boils from the sole of his foot to the crown of his head" (Job 2:7). Why did God ever allow Satan to afflict Job with such a horrible plague or pestilence? We live in a world separated from God's original plan of complete health and wholeness. It is a world of pathogens, viruses, and germs. A world in which pestilences and plagues devastate entire communities and impact whole countries. God does not always intervene to prevent Satan's attacks, but through it all He is with us. He is there to strengthen, encourage, and support us. It is often through life's toughest times that we seek God most earnestly and long for heaven more deeply.

There's a second way that the word "pestilence" is used in the Bible. At times pestilences are the judgments of God upon the wicked. At times the Old Testament prophets describe pestilences as God's means of leading His rebellious people to repentance. The prophets Jeremiah and Ezekiel use the word 25 times in harmony with God's judgments. You may say that's rather strange, but think about Egypt. Were the plagues of ancient Egypt simply natural disasters, or were they God's judgments to deliver His people? In love God sent warning after warning to the Egyptians. He graciously sent repeated messages to them to avoid the disaster that was coming, but they willfully refused His loving invitations, and the judgments of God fell upon the land. Love speaks gently, but it also speaks in thunderous tones at times to get our attention. God's ultimate purpose in all our life experiences is to lead us closer to Him.

There is a third use of the word "pestilence." At times God simply withdraws His protective power. There are times God withdraws His presence and allows the natural result of sin to take place. Do you remember the story of Israel being bitten by snakes in the wilderness? Many died of the venom. God simply withdrew His presence to allow the consequence of their sinful choices to be played out so they would turn in repentance to His will. When we see pestilences raging in our land, it may be God's clarion call for us to become more serious about our commitment to Christ, experience a deeper repentance, and surrender our lives fully to Him.

John the revelator gives us further insight on the restraining power of God. Speaking of the calamities that will come in the last days, he declares, "After these things I saw four angels standing at the four corners of the earth, holding the four winds of the earth, that the wind should not blow on the earth, on the sea, and on any tree. Then I saw another angel ascending from the east, having the seal of the living God. And he cried with a loud voice to the four angels to whom it was granted to harm the earth and the sea, saying, "Do not harm the earth, the sea, or the trees till we have sealed the servants of our God on their foreheads" (Revelation 7:1-3). In the prophetic language of the Bible, wind represents destruction. Think of the destructive force of a tornado or a hurricane. Revelation pictures the angels of God holding back the destruction that will come upon the earth just before Jesus returns. The famines, earthquakes, fires, floods, and pestilences we see all around us are a foretaste of what is coming. The angels are restraining the full force of destruction while the Holy Spirit powerfully appeals to people everywhere to make a full commitment to Jesus.

God is preparing His people for the final crisis that is soon to break upon this world. Jesus appeals to us to make a total, absolute commitment to Him, to be anchored in His Word, and to be filled with His love so that all the demons in hell with their devilish schemes cannot move us. We will not be shaken, because He cannot be shaken, and our eyes are fixed upon Him.

Rising Natural Disasters

Jesus describes natural disasters, including pestilences, that devastate the earth in the context of the signs of His second coming. Let me hasten to add that we need to avoid two extremes. One extreme is the fanaticism that shouts, "The coronavirus is here, so Jesus must be coming next week [or next month or next year]." There are some people who are consumed with fanciful, sensational time-setting theories not found in the Bible. The other extreme is to dismiss this virus as some natural phenomenon that will soon pass, that has absolutely nothing at all to do with last-day signs. But that's certainly not what Jesus said. In Matthew 24 Jesus discusses end-time signs and declares, "For nation will rise against nation, and kingdom against kingdom. And there will be famines, pestilences, and earthquakes in various places. All these are the beginning of sorrows" (Matthew 24:7, 8). Jesus lists wars, rumors of war, the rise of nations against nations, kingdoms fighting against kingdoms as part of an end-time scenario. He adds natural disasters such as earthquakes, famines, and pestilences among the more than 20 signs He foretells in Matthew 24. The Gospel of Luke also speaks about these end-time signs. Luke was a medical doctor and is very precise in reporting Jesus' description of final events. In Luke 21 Jesus plainly states, "And there will be great earthquakes in various places, and famines and pestilences; and there will be fearful sights and great signs from heaven" (Luke 21:11). Jesus predicted that there would be dramatic signs in the natural world that would be a sign of His return.

It might seem strange to talk about famines today in a world in which so many people are obese, but it is a fact that millions starve to death every year. The United Nations Food and Agriculture Organization estimates that nearly 870 million people are suffering from chronic undernourishment. That represents one of eight people living on the planet, or about 13 percent of the world's population. Every day more than 20,000 people die from the effects of malnutrition. That is almost 7.5 million people every year.

Jesus said there would be famines, earthquakes, and pestilences. The number of earthquakes measuring 3.0 or more on the Richter scale has been significant. Meanwhile, tsunamis, mudslides, avalanches, tornadoes, and volcanic eruptions have been breaking all previous records for their violence and disastrous effects. More than $24 billion of weather damage is caused each year. It is as if all nature is speaking, saying, "Lord, it's time for You to come and deliver us."

The 2004 Sumatra-Andaman earthquake and the Indonesian tsunami that followed had waves almost 100 feet high and took more than 225,000 lives, with thousands more injured. In the earthquake that struck the Sichuan province of China on May 12, 2008, almost

70,000 people died and another 18,000 were listed as missing. On January 12, 2010, Haiti was struck by a major quake. According to Haitian government figures, at least 220,000 people died and more than 3 million were seriously affected. On March 11, 2011, a 9.0 earthquake caused a tsunami that struck Japan and killed almost 20,000 people. Earthquakes have been prevalent in the past 50 years. Jesus also predicted the rise of pestilences.

Pestilences are epidemics that impact entire countries. Pestilences can also be categorized as strange diseases that destroy our crops; pollutants that impact the environment; or noxious substances that contaminate our air and water.

Why do we spray our crops with deadly chemicals called pesticides? Because if we didn't, the pestilences, or the pests, would destroy them! You can hardly find anything in the supermarket that's not covered with pesticides. Agriculture around the world uses 5.6 billion pounds of toxic pollutants per year. These pesticides run off into our land and into waterways and oceans. This insatiable desire to make money by rapidly producing crops and quickly ripening them by artificial fertilizers to get them on the market sooner is having devastating consequences on the environment and our health.

A group of scientists got together and issued what they called a "Warning to Humanity." They wrote: "No more than one or a few decades remain." Now, this is not some preacher standing in a pulpit; it is a group of scientists. They said: "No more than one or a few decades remain before the chance to avert the threats we now confront will be lost and the prospects of humanity immeasurably diminished." They are talking about global warming, the greenhouse effect. They are talking about vehicles and industry emitting toxic carbon pollutants into the atmosphere, the melting of the polar caps and the rise of the oceans. This is not somebody crying wolf! The danger we face is real.

We are seeing another form of pestilence in the new diseases that are springing up around the world. Have you wondered about new epidemics? Where are they coming from? Before science can find a solution or a vaccine for one, another appears. Just think about the pestilences that have taken millions of lives in recent years. We have had mad cow disease, bird flu, HIV/AIDS, Lyme disease, the Marburg virus, the West Nile virus, Ebola, coronaviruses, including SARS and now COVID-19.

A Sign of Christ's Return?

Does that mean that this COVID-19 virus that has ravaged the world is a sign of Christ's coming? It does not stand alone as the sign. But when you look at the larger picture, pestilences are one of multiple signs that Jesus predicts will occur preliminary to His return. These events indicate that the time is running out and that we are living on the verge of eternity. The stage is being set for the climactic events described in the prophetic books of Daniel and Revelation to soon be fulfilled.

In the light of Christ's predictions in His prophetic Word, what can we expect in the future? Natural disasters will increase. Famines, earthquakes, and pestilences will escalate. Just as in Noah's day, when a sinful world full of immorality and violence filled the cup of its iniquity in rebellion against God and the floodwaters deluged this world, so our world is preparing for God's final judgments. God lovingly appeals to a wayward planet. There is nothing more important to God than saving as many people as possible. When God withdraws His protective power, natural disasters and death dealing disease run rampant. God does not cause these disasters, but uses them to appeal to us on the fragility of life. They drive us to our knees to seek the only source of security, which is in Christ and the promises of His Word. The Bible is a book filled with the hopeful promises of God.

Hope Makes a Difference

When we lose hope, dark clouds of despair hang over our heads. The future appears gloomy, and everything about tomorrow seems uncertain. But hope leads us from what is to what can be. It paints tomorrow in an array of bright colors. It lifts our spirits from the mud below to the heavens above.

Hope is not some idle wish or vague longing for a better future. It is not baseless desire or an uncertain expectation with no real certainty or assurance. In the ancient Scriptures hope is a strong, confident expectation based on the unchangeable promises of God with the certainty that the thing you hope for will be accomplished. The apostle Paul, writing in the Bible book of Romans, states that the "things were written aforetime were written for our learning, that we through patience and comfort of the scriptures might have hope" (Romans 15:4, KJV).

The apostle Paul faced life's fiercest trials. He was stoned, beaten, unjustly condemned, and imprisoned. But he writes to the believers in Rome who were living through trying times: "Now may the God of hope fill you with all joy and peace in believing, that you may abound in hope by the power of the Holy Spirit" (verse 13). God is a God of hope. As we grasp His loving concern for us in all the circumstances of life, our hearts will be filled with joy and peace, and we will abound in hope.

The promises of God reveal hope for today, tomorrow, and forever. They speak with certainty in an uncertain world. They encourage our hearts and give us the sense that we are not alone in this world. They speak hope to our troubled minds and peace to our anxious spirits.

Although we may face challenges, and life might not go as we have planned or desired, the promises of God are sure. Our happiness is not based on the illusionary idea that nothing bad will ever happen to us. It is not based on the mythical dream that each day is brighter than the day before. Sometimes bad things happen to good people.

We live in a broken world. Sickness, suffering, poverty, and disease afflict both the righteous and the unrighteous, but here is the difference: Those who put their faith in God are filled with hope. Our hope is anchored in a God who will never let us down (see Hebrews 6:18). It is rooted in a God who is there in our trials, with us in our difficulties. It has as its foundation a Christ who once dwelt in human flesh, one who understands us and strengthens us in all our trials (see Hebrews 4:15). He identifies with us in our tears and comforts our hearts. He came to provide us with the hope of a better tomorrow.

Hope for Troubled Times

Today let your heart be filled with hope. One day soon Jesus will come, and the heartaches and trials, the challenges and difficulties of life, will be over, and we will live with Him forever.

CHAPTER 2

OVERCOMING FEAR, WORRY, AND ANXIETY

Someone has said that fear, worry, and anxiety are our greatest enemies. Recently I read a fascinating story: "According to an ancient legend, a peasant man driving one day to Constantinople was stopped by an old woman, who asked him for a ride. He took her up beside him, and as they drove along, he looked at her, became frightened, and asked, 'Who are you?'

"The old woman replied, 'I am Cholera.'

"Frightened, the peasant ordered the old woman to get down and walk, but she persuaded him to take her along, upon her promise that she would not kill more than five people in Constantinople. As a pledge of the promise she handed him a dagger, saying to him that it was the only weapon with which she could be killed. Then she added: 'I shall meet you in two days. If I break my promise, you may stab me.'

"In Constantinople 120 people died of the cholera. The enraged man who had driven her to the city searched for her. When he found her, he raised the dagger that she had given him to kill her. He shouted, 'You promised that you would not kill more than five people, and 120 died.'

"But she stopped him, saying: 'I have kept my agreement. I killed only five. Fear killed the others.'

"This legend is a true parable of life." Disease may kill thousands of people, but thousands more die because they are overwhelmed by fear. When we look to the future with fear, expecting the worst rather than with confidence expecting the best, we become crippled with anxiety and paralyzed with worry. From the time we are born until the day we die, fear often casts its dark shadow on our lives. Fear crushes our spirit, breaks down our immune system, weakens our will, and renders us powerless in our battle with the enemy. Fear strangles our joy and destroys our dreams.

Fear is a strong emotion closely related to anxiety and worry. It often occurs as the result of some threat, situation, or danger that is apparently unavoidable. One thing we learned from COVID-19 is how suddenly a pandemic can strike fear in the heart of an entire nation. People became fearful that each person they met might be carrying the coronavirus and infect them. Each cough created anxiety that they might have the virus. Every time they sneezed, their hearts beat faster. They continually asked themselves, "Do I have the virus? And if I do, is it my death sentence?"

Dealing With Fear

What can deliver us from our worst fears, or it might be more accurate to say who can deliver us from those fears? The ancient Scriptures are filled with more than 3,000 promises of God's love and care. Many of the Bible's promises are specifically encouraging in times of crisis. Clinging to the promises of God, we are filled with hope when we face catastrophes. We confront them with confidence in Christ, who stands by our side. We have the assurance of the One who said, "I will never leave you nor forsake you" (Hebrews 13:5). One of the great Bible stories on overcoming fear takes place in an oft-forgotten story tucked away in the Bible's Old Testament. The king of Syria had surrounded the Israelite city of Dothan. The king's intent was to capture Elisha. Every time the King of Syria had made a battle move, the prophet Elisha had warned the captain of Israel's armies. The Syrian king was furious. The only way he could win the battle was to capture and kill Elisha. He brought all the forces in his mighty army to surround the city so that escape was impossible. When Elisha's servant woke early in the morning and saw the city surrounded by the enemy armies with hundreds of horses and chariots, he was seized with fear. Worry filled his heart. Death seemed inevitable. Trembling with terror, he came to Elisha. He was so worried that it was difficult for him to speak, but finally the words came out: "Alas, my master! What shall we do?" (2 Kings 6:15). Elisha's answer is classic. It provides a life-changing principle for all those who are gripped by fear. It gives comfort to those who are consumed by worry and anxiety. Elisha simply stated, "Do not fear, for those who are with us are more than those who are with them" (verse 17). Despite an almost impossible situation, God was still in control. He was still on His throne. He had a solution where there appeared to be no solution. He could make a way where there seemed to be no way.

Elisha prayed that his young servant would see—the angelic armies of heaven surrounding them, protecting them, and eventually delivering them. Miraculously God struck the Syrian armies with blindness, and Elisha and his servant escaped. God has a thousand ways to deliver us from our worst fears. If our eyes are focused on the problem, fear will overcome us. If our eyes are fixed upon Jesus, the emotion of fear may still be present, but it will not cripple us. Fear will no longer dominate our lives.

The answer to crippling fear is not that we will never be afraid—it is rather that we have One with us in our fears, strengthening us to go on no matter how we feel. We have One who is larger than our fears, bigger than our worries, and greater than our anxieties by our side, and He has practical, down-to-earth, real solutions to our problems. The sense of the presence of God is the antidote to fear. We were created to live by faith, not be consumed by our fears. E. Stanley Jones, a popular twentieth-century preacher, once said, "I am inwardly fashioned for faith, not for fear. Fear is not my native land; faith is. I am so made that worry and anxiety are sand in the machinery of life; faith is the oil. I live better by faith and confidence than by fear, doubt, and anxiety. In anxiety and worry, my being is gasping for breath—these are not my native air. But in faith and confidence, I breathe freely—these are my native air." We were created to live a life of trust in the One who made us. Look beyond your fears to the Christ, who cares for you more than you will ever know.

Faith Versus Fear

There is another fear breaker found in a story on the stormy sea of Galilee that teaches us the importance of faith, not fear. The Sea of Galilee is about 13 miles long and eight miles wide. At times fierce winds blow in and quickly turn the once-calm sea into a torrent of raging fury. As Jesus' disciples crossed the sea on a starlit night, the waters were calm. Suddenly inky-black clouds filled the sky. The winds whipped the waves into a fury. Huge waves crashed against the boat. Matthew's Gospel puts it this way: "But the boat was now in the middle of the sea, tossed by the waves, for the wind was contrary. Now in the fourth watch of the night Jesus went to them, walking on the sea" (Matthew 14:24, 25). The fourth watch of the night is between 3:00 a.m. and 6:00 a.m. in the morning. They set sail in the early evening. They could have made it across the sea in two or three hours, but they battled the wind and waves for eight long hours. Evidently the wind blew against them, and they were no closer to their destination than when they started. They were weary, tired, and exhausted. They felt they could battle no longer. Their strength was gone. There are times in life when the battle is fierce. The storms rage all around us, and we are so exhausted with the battle that we feel we cannot fight any longer. Here is the incredible good news.

Where was Jesus during this time? What was He doing during their intense struggle? He was praying for them. He was asking the Father to increase their faith, to give them strength to face the storm, to give them the courage to go on. Jesus knew what they did not know: the cross was coming, and the storm that they were going through now would increase their faith for what would lie ahead. In the storms of life that we face daily, Jesus is preparing us for greater crises that will break upon our world in the future.

The disciples saw the storm; Jesus saw them. Their eyes were fixed upon the waves; Jesus' eyes were fixed upon them. To the disciples everything seemed out of control, but Jesus was still in control. Amid the storms of life His eyes are upon us. When the thunder roars and the waves are high, He is still mighty to save. In the darkness He is our light of life.

In verses 25, 26 the scripture says, "Now in the fourth watch of the night Jesus went to them, walking on the sea. And when the disciples saw Him walking on the sea, they were troubled, saying, 'It is a ghost!' And they cried out for fear." The Greek word for "fear" translated in verse 26 is an extremely strong word. It can be better translated "terrified." Here is the problem. The disciples feared what they did not know. They saw what they thought was a ghost. Belief in evil spirits was common in first-century Palestine. The idea of ghosts, goblins, and phantoms was widespread. These disciples had spent years with Jesus, but in a time of storm their fears overtook their rational thinking processes. The unknown often creates fear, and the problem is that sometimes our worst fears come true. There are those who say, "Don't worry about it. Everything is going to be OK." But you and I know that everything may not always turn out as we desire, so we play the "what if" game: What if I do have cancer? How will I handle it if my physician tells me I must begin treatment immediately? My husband was not home for supper at 5:00 p.m., and it is 7:00 p.m., and he has not called. What if he has been in an accident? My company is making severe cutbacks. What if I lose my job and can't pay my bills? My teenage son is on a camping trip. It has been three days, and he has not called. What if he is lost in the mountains?

The "what if" questions must give way to the voice of Christ, who proclaims in the midst of the raging sea, the blowing winds, and the overwhelming darkness, "Be of good cheer! It is I; do not be afraid" (verse 27). Have you ever noticed how many times Jesus says, "Be of good cheer"? Throughout the Gospels Jesus uses the expressions "Be of good cheer" and "Do not be afraid" repeatedly.

Jesus is the answer to the overwhelming fears that consume our energy, rob our joy, and ruin our health. Fear must give way to faith as we adjust our focus. Fear is an emotion. We cannot necessarily control our emotions. Emotions come and go. They often suddenly sweep over us. Faith is an attitude. Faith is trust in God as a well-known friend, believing that He loves us and will never do us any harm.

A Personal Illustration

Let me give you a very personal illustration of trust. It was necessary for me to get some medical treatments for a particular condition I am facing. One of the treatments my medical team recommended was hyperbaric oxygen. This necessitated being placed in a hyperbaric oxygen chamber for about two hours per day for 35 to 40 treatments. When the owner of the clinic explained the treatment to me, he said the problem many people have going into this chamber is not claustrophobia; it is trust. After you are placed in the chamber, there is no way you can get out alone. You must have absolute confidence that the chamber operator will get you out when your treatment is over. If you trust the operator, you will be fine. When I entered that hyperbaric oxygen chamber, I placed my trust in the medical technician. I had no fear, because I had confidence in the one who was operating the machine. I believed the one in charge knew what he was doing. As we enter trying experiences, as fears arise, as anxiety threatens our joy, we can have absolute confidence in Christ. He is the one in charge, and He knows what He is doing.

The answer to the fears in our life is faith—faith that Jesus is there in the storms of life and will take us through any situation and get us out the other side. Fear is an emotion. Faith is an attitude, and focus is a choice.

Peter did not allow his fears to overwhelm his faith so that he would lose focus. Amid the storm and the raging waves, Peter cried out to Jesus, "Lord, if it is You, command me to come to You on the water (verse 28). Faith leads us out of the boat. Faith leads us to walk on the stormy seas with Jesus. Faith leads us to face the winds and rain with our eyes fixed on the Master of the wind and the Lord of the heaven and the earth. Faith triumphs over fear. Trust triumphs over our trials. Faith overcomes the obstacles in our way and enables us to walk on stormy seas with Jesus.

Jesus responded to Peter's request with one word: "Come" (verse 29). Jesus never says, "Stay away." Jesus never says, "You deal with it." Jesus never says, "That's your problem, not Mine." Jesus never says, "Stop troubling Me with that. I have got enough big problems to deal with in the world."

Jesus says come . . . step out of the boat. Come by faith and walk on the water. Come, My arms are strong. You are not going to drown. Peter responded to Christ's invitation and stepped out of the boat. He ventured out into the unknown with Christ. He flung himself into the jaws of death. In the face of the howling wind, Peter did not allow his fears to paralyze him. What are your greatest fears? What do you worry about most? Christ is greater than our fears. He is bigger than our doubts. He is larger than our questions. He invites us to come to Him in the stormy seas of life.

When Peter kept his eyes fixed on Jesus, he walked on water, but something happened to him that often happens to us in the storms of life. Peter lost his sense of focus. Verse 30 adds: "But when he saw that the wind was boisterous, he was afraid." When Peter kept his eyes fixed upon Christ and trusted His word, he walked on water. When he focused on the waves and the treacherous situation he was in, he sank. Either we look at our difficulties from an earthly perspective with our human reason and weakness, or we look through the eyes of faith at the promises of God.

When we are dominated by fear, we sink, and the sinking of our spirits is the result of the sinking of our faith. We fear when we forget. When Peter began to sink beneath the stormy sea, there was only one thing that saved him. It was not his skill as an experienced fisherman. It was not his knowledge of the Sea of Galilee. It was not his wisdom in solving problems. It was not his ability to swim back to the boat. As Peter began to sink, he cried out, "Lord, save me!" (verse 30).

Matthew: An Eyewitness of a Miracle

Matthew was an eyewitness of this miracle. He writes from firsthand experience. Matthew was in the boat watching the entire scene play out. He writes, "And immediately Jesus stretched out His hand and caught him" (Matthew 14:31). When Peter cried out, Jesus immediately responded. Jesus is there in the storms of life. He is there when the waves are high and the night is dark.

Did you notice in these passages there are two cries? The cry of fear and the cry of faith. When the disciples saw what they believed was an apparition, according to verse 26 they cried out in fear. When Peter was sinking in the waves, he cried out in faith.

We can have absolute confidence that Jesus never turns away from those who cry out in faith. His arm is strong to hold us up. David describes this beautifully in the Psalms: "Now I know that the Lord saves His anointed . . . with the saving strength of His right hand" (Psalm 20:6). We are safe in the hands of Jesus.

Now, notice what Jesus does not say to Peter. He does not say, "Peter, where is your faith?" or "Peter, you have no faith." He says, "O you of little faith" (Matthew 14:31). A little faith is better than no faith. It reminds me of Jesus' statement in Matthew 17:20: "If you have faith as a mustard seed, you will say to this mountain"—this mountain of difficulty, this mountain of problems, this mountain of trouble— " 'Move . . . ,' and it will move." When we exercise the little faith we have, our faith in Christ's power to get us through the storms of life will grow into a mighty force that enables us to walk on the stormy seas of life's challenges.

Notice this point: Peter had enough faith to get out of the boat, but not enough to get through the storm. Jesus often allows the storms of life to blow upon us to increase our faith. If we would believe more, we would doubt less. The work of faith is to resolve our doubts, so we place our confidence in Christ and Christ alone.

Whether we are consumed with fear or filled with hope all depends on where we are looking. If we are looking at our problems or the problems of this world, our hearts will be filled with fear. Jesus says, "Look up!" Why? When we look to heaven's sanctuary, we see Jesus and discover strength in His promises. In Christ we find confidence. In Christ we experience assurance. In Christ we are lifted above life's uncertainties and concerns, and our hearts are filled with security in the One who loves us with an everlasting, undying, unfathomable, exhaustless, endless love.

Trusting God's Promises

The Bible says "Do not fear" or "Fear not" repeatedly. Although I have not personally counted the number of times the Bible uses this expression, one author has counted 365 times that "fear not" or similar expressions are used throughout the Bible—that is one for every day of the year. God has the entire calendar year covered. He invites us to rest in His love, trust in His grace, and rejoice in His power.

In one of the Bible's most reassuring promises, Isaiah encourages us by echoing the words of our Lord: "Fear not, for I am with you." Why don't we fear? Jesus is with us. Whatever we must go through, He is by our side. "Fear not, for I am with you; be not dismayed, for I am your God. I will strengthen you, yes, I will help you, I will uphold you with My righteous right hand" (Isaiah 41:10). When we see sickness and suffering and disease all around us, we need not fear, because Jesus is with us. Earlier in the book of Isaiah the inspired Word states, "Say to those who are fearful-hearted, 'Be strong, do not fear! Behold, your God will come with vengeance, with the recompense of God; He will come and save you'" (Isaiah 35:4). Why don't we need to fear? The reason we are not afraid is not that we believe we will never get sick. We are free from paralyzing fear because we believe that whatever state we find ourselves in, Christ will be with us. You remember that Job experienced a terrible pestilence that horribly afflicted his body. During his suffering he cried out in confidence, "For I know that my Redeemer lives, and He shall stand at last on the earth; and after my skin is destroyed, this I know, that in my flesh I shall see God" (Job 19:25). Job had the absolute assurance that a better day was coming and that one day he would see God face to face. Until then with hope and assurance he could exclaim, "Though He slay me, yet will I trust Him" (Job 13:15). Job lived a life of trust in the God who promised that He would be with him each moment of the day and who promised him that a better tomorrow was coming.

Even if we develop a life-threatening disease, our faith clings to His promise that one day Jesus will come again to take us home. Like Job, we believe that one day we will see Him face to face. Jesus speaks these reassuring words to us: "Let not your heart be troubled; you believe in God, believe also in Me. In My Father's house are many mansions; if it were not so, I would have told you. I go to prepare a place for you. And if I go and prepare a place for you, I will come again and receive you to Myself; that where I am, there you may be also" (John 14:1-3). One day Jesus will come again. And on that wonderful day we will be caught up in the clouds in the sky to meet Him in the air. Sickness and suffering will be eradicated forever. Disease and death will be eradicated in the presence of our loving God.

Hope for Troubled Times

One of the major reasons we do not live in fear is that we know the end game. We know that sickness will not have the last word: Christ will. We know the coronavirus, or any other virus, natural disaster, calamity, or nuclear war, will not destroy all life on Planet Earth. We have the promise of Jesus' return. We see famines. We see earthquakes. We see distress of nations. We see the rise of nuclear war. We see the potential of nuclear disaster. We see climate change. We see pestilences taking the lives of thousands.

We see these things, but we have a hope that enables us to thrive in life's toughest times. There is a sense of confidence that takes us through, because we've read the last chapters of the Bible. We know how the story ends. In Revelation 21:4, 5 John writes, "And God will wipe away every tear from their eyes; there shall be no more death, nor sorrow, nor crying. There shall be no more pain, for the former things have passed away. Then He who sat on the throne said, 'Behold, I make all things new.' " We believe in the blessed hope in Titus 2:13 that Christ is coming again. So we look beyond what is to what will be. We look beyond today to tomorrow. We look beyond sickness to health. We look beyond the pestilences that are carried through the air to the pure air where there will be no more pestilences.

God has a purpose in permitting these calamities to occur. He is calling us to totally, completely depend upon Him. He is revealing to us that there is no certainty in the world we live in. Christ is our assurance. He is our security. He is our Savior, our Redeemer, our Deliverer, our coming King. What does this virus do when we see it spreading so rapidly? It calls us to our senses.

This world is not all that there is. Christ is speaking to you and to me. Our lives are fragile. Every single one of us lives in these fragile earthen bodies. But beyond what is, there is something better yet coming—and that is the glory of Christ. There is something worth living for beyond this life, and that's Jesus Christ. Allow Him to fill your heart, to take away your fears, strengthen your resolve, and prepare you for His soon return.

CHAPTER 3

DISCOVERED: THE ULTIMATE VACCINE

Research laboratories and university medical centers throughout the United States and around the world are racing at breakneck speed to find an effective vaccine for the coronavirus COVID-19. These trial vaccines are designed to produce a strong immune response, including an increased production of antibodies and protection that will last longer against viral and bacterial infections.

The University of Nebraska is part of a global hunt for the much-needed protection against a virus that has played havoc with the world economy, forced people into self-quarantine, and infected millions of people. As countries have attempted to control the spread of this deadly pandemic, one of the larger concerns that has surfaced is the fear that a second round of COVID-19 might strike within a short time. This concern has caused researchers to place top priority on developing a vaccine as quickly as possible.

The U.S. National Institutes of Health (NIH) is coordinating its work with laboratories, universities, and research institutes in a frantic attempt to discover a vaccine. They have begun their first trial studies in Seattle, Washington. Presently, about two thirds of that study's participants have gotten the first of two needed doses. Forty healthy volunteers at the Kansas City research lab and the University of Pennsylvania have also begun clinic trials using this vaccine. One medical pharmaceutical company, Inovio, is working with Chinese researchers to also begin a similar study in that country soon. These early-stage studies are a first step to see if a vaccine appears safe enough for larger tests needed to prove whether it will protect against the virus.

One group of United States researchers are experimenting with a different type of COVID-19 vaccine. This one injects the vaccine serum into the arm much like a simple skin test. "It's the most important trial that we've ever done," Dr. John Ervin of the Center for Pharmaceutical Research told the Associated Press. Even if the research goes well, it is expected to take more than a year before any vaccine could be widely available. Dozens of potential vaccines are being designed in labs around the world, for which the testing process is expected to begin during the next several months.

"The good thing is we've got a bunch of candidates," Dr. Anthony Fauci, the NIH's infectious diseases chief, said during a podcast for the *Journal of the American Medical Association*. One of the leading researchers in this field made this fascinating statement: "People are beating down the door to get into this trial."

People are so afraid of this deadly, rapidly spreading virus that they are anxious to get a vaccine that will prevent them from contracting COVID-19. Although this present pandemic has caused hundreds of thousands of deaths around the world, there is another virus that has infested humanity that is even more deadly. COVID-19 may destroy your body, but this fatal disease can take more than your physical life. Jesus made this remarkable statement: "And do not fear those who kill the body but cannot kill the soul. But rather fear Him who is able to destroy both soul and body in hell" (Matthew 10:28). The virus of sin is much more deadly than the coronavirus. COVID-19 can destroy the body, but sin can destroy our body and soul. Once infected with the virus of sin, the prognosis is death, unless a vaccine can be found. How did this pandemic begin, and what is the ultimate solution to the sin problem?

Another More Deadly Virus

God created human beings in His image, but when Adam and Eve listened to the voice of the evil one in the Garden of Eden and yielded to his temptations, the virus of sin was passed from them to their descendants. This is why the prophet Jeremiah declares, "The heart is deceitful above all things, and desperately wicked" (Jeremiah 17:9). Isaiah adds, "All we like sheep have gone astray; we have turned, every one, to his own way" (Isaiah 53:6). And do you remember the lament of the apostle Paul when he cried out, "O wretched man that I am! Who shall deliver me from this body of death?" (Romans 7:24). We have a disease that is fatal. It's deadly, but just like so many people with the coronavirus who were asymptomatic, we walk around spreading the virus of sin to others without even realizing it at times.

There were many people during the height of this COVID-19 epidemic who apparently had no initial symptoms. They did not have a sore throat or a fever. They did not have fatigue or a cough. They appeared normal, but were walking around infecting others. Sometimes these people never showed signs of the disease, or developed only mild symptoms. But in others the disease burst upon them with its full force. Their temperature rose, their breathing became labored, their bodies weak. They were fighting for their lives. The best efforts of the most outstanding medical personnel were powerless to save them. There was no medical remedy for the coronavirus, but thank God there is a remedy for the virus of sin.

The Divine Physician's Prescription

There is One who can deliver us from sin's clutches. When the apostle Paul cries out, "O wretched man that I am! Who will deliver me from this body of death?" he does not leave us with a lingering question. He answers his own question by triumphantly declaring, "I thank God—through Jesus Christ our Lord" (Romans 7:24, 25). There is a Physician who has the remedy for the virus of sin. Jesus plunged into this cesspool of sin to meet the emergency. The Divine Physician entered the arena of human affairs with the antibodies to deliver us from sin's virus. He came to this snake pit of a fallen world with all its deadly venom, met the temptations of Satan head-on, and was victorious. He satisfied the demands of the law that we have broken. He died the death that was ours so we could live the life that was His. The cross reveals to the entire universe the depths Christ would go to save us.

Concerning Christ, the Scriptures state, "Who Himself bore our sins in His own body on the tree" (1 Peter 2:24). The cross of Calvary reveals a love beyond human comprehension. Looking at the crucified Son of God, we can say with the apostle Paul, He "loved me and gave Himself for me" (Galatians 2:20). Christ's grace is unmerited, undeserved, and unearned. Jesus died the agonizing, painful death that lost sinners will die. He experienced the fullness of the Father's wrath or judgment against sin. He was rejected so that we could be accepted. He died the death that was ours so that we could live the life that was His. He wore the crown of thorns so that we could wear a crown of glory. He was nailed upright in torturous pain upon a cross so that we could reign on a throne with the redeemed of all ages. He wore the robe of shame so that we could wear royal robes forever.

Marvel of all marvels, wonder of all wonders, in our shame and guilt Jesus did not reject us, He reached out in love to accept us. He is the "Lamb of God who takes away the sin of the world" (John 1:29). In the ancient sanctuary of the Old Testament, the dying lamb represented the broken, bruised, battered, bloody body of our Savior. Rightly understood, these sacrifices point forward to an old rugged cross. They speak of the nails and the crown of thorns. They speak of the farce of a trial, the agony of the tree, the ridicule of the Roman soldiers, and the taunts of the crowd. They speak of the cost of sin, the condemnation of the law, and the marvel of grace.

The cross speaks of a love so marvelous, so amazing, so divine, that it would rather take the condemnation, guilt, and penalty of sin upon itself than have even one of His children eternally lost. There is an insightful statement in *The Desire of Ages*, a book that reveals the depths of Christ's sacrifice. "Satan with his fierce temptations wrung the heart of Jesus. The Savior could not see through the portals of the tomb. Hope did not present to Him His coming forth from the grave a conqueror, or tell Him of the Father's acceptance of the sacrifice. He feared that sin was so offensive to God that Their separation was to be eternal. Christ felt the anguish that the sinner will feel when mercy shall no longer plead for the guilty race. It was the sense of sin, bringing the Father's wrath upon Him as [the sinner's] substitute, that made the cup He drank so bitter, and broke the heart of the Son of God" (Ellen G. White, *The Desire of Ages*, p. 753).

This is the story of grace. This is the story of a Savior's love beyond measure. This is the story of a Jesus who loves us so much that He would rather experience hell itself then have one of us lost. This is the story of a boundless, unfathomable, incomprehensible, undying, unending, infinite love that longs for us to be with Him eternally. It is the story of the divine Son of God who was willing to assume the guilt, condemnation, and consequences of our sin, and to be separated from His Father forever, if that is what it took to save us. Christ's death on the cross delivers us from sin's condemnation, guilt, shame, and ultimate penalty. The shed blood of Christ is the only effective vaccine for the virus of sin. But the story does not end at the cross.

Jesus Is Alive

If Jesus died and never rose again, He would be merely a martyr dying for a good cause. If He never conquered the tomb, what hope would we have of eternal life? It takes both the dying Christ and the living Christ to redeem us. The resurrected Christ delivers from sin's grip. Sin's dominion in our lives has been broken. It no longer holds us in its clutches. There is a power stronger than the influence of our heredity, our environment, or our past mistakes; it is the power of the living Christ, risen from the dead, changing our lives. If Christ's tomb were not empty, our lives could not be full. If His body were still in the tomb, there would be no assurance that our bodies could ever leave the tomb. If He were not resurrected, we would have little hope of resurrection.

Here is the incredibly good news: The evidence of the literal, bodily resurrection of Christ is strong. In Matthew's Gospel we read, "The next day, the one after Preparation Day, the chief priests and the Pharisees went to Pilate. 'Sir,' they said, 'we remember that while he was still alive that deceiver said, "After three days I will rise again." So give the order for the tomb to be made secure until the third day. Otherwise, his disciples may come and steal the body and tell the people that he has been raised from the dead. This last deception will be worse than the first.'

" 'Take a guard,' Pilate answered. 'Go, make the tomb as secure as you know how.' So they went and made the tomb secure by putting a seal on the stone and posting the guard" (Matthew 27:62-68, NIV).

Remember that Matthew was a tax collector, so we can expect him to be very detailed. Notice Pilate's words: "Make the tomb as secure as you know how." Here are four crucial points in this passage.

1. The scribes and Pharisees were concerned about Christ's resurrection.
2. Pilate ordered a Roman guard to watch the tomb.
3. A large stone was rolled over the entrance.
4. A Roman seal secured the tomb.

A Roman guard of hardened, battle-tested soldiers was stationed to guard the tomb. This contingent of Roman soldiers was honor-bound to protect the sepulcher. Roman military protocol demanded faithfulness to an assigned task. Any deviation from absolute loyalty and a failure to accomplish the assigned mission was punishable by death. Then we have the issue of the Roman seal. The soldiers affixed the Roman seal on the tomb, which was meant to prevent any attempt at vandalizing the sepulcher. The seal stood for the power and authority of the Roman Empire. Anyone trying to remove the stone from the tomb's entrance would have broken the seal and thus incurred the wrath of Roman law. The Romans ruled Jerusalem with an iron fist and did not tolerate any challenge to Rome's authority.

Can any logical mind think that the disciples would challenge the authority of Rome after the Roman government put Jesus to death? Where were the disciples at this time? They were cowering in fear in the upper room. Peter had just denied his Lord three times. At the cross the disciples forsook Jesus and fled. It is illogical to think that these faithless disciples would have the courage to break the Roman seal. Then there is the matter of the moving of the stone. In John 20:1 the Scripture records: "Now the first day of the week Mary Magdalene went to the tomb early, while it was still dark, and saw that the stone had been taken away from the tomb." Ancient tombs at this time were about four feet wide and five feet high. Archaeologists have discovered a number of these tombs around Jerusalem. Typically, one of these gravestones weighed about two tons. It would sit in a groove in front of the entrance to the tomb and be rolled into place by a lever to secure the tomb. Often the groove was not level, so the round stone was gently rolled down a very slight incline into place. Once the tomb was secure, it was extremely difficult to move the stone, because you would have to roll it back up the incline.

Josh McDowell makes a good point when he asserts that "so many security precautions were taken with the trial, crucifixion, burial, entombment, sealing, and guarding of Christ's tomb that it becomes very difficult for critics to defend their position that Christ did not rise from the dead."

Where were the disciples when Mary first approached the tomb? They were hiding in an upper room, afraid that they may be hunted and killed next. One of the greatest evidences of the resurrection of Christ is the transformation in the lives of the disciples when they powerfully proclaimed His resurrection. Where did they go first? They went back to Jerusalem, the very place they had fled from. Eventually every one of these disciples, except John, died a martyr's death. James was beheaded. Peter was crucified upside down. It is preposterous to think this group of disciples would die for a lie they themselves had manufactured.

Historian Paul Maier observes that "if all the evidence is weighed carefully and fairly, it is indeed justifiable, according to the canons of historical research, to conclude that the sepulcher of Joseph of Arimathea, in which Jesus was buried, was actually empty on the morning of the first Easter. And no shred of evidence has yet been discovered in literary sources, epigraphy, or archaeology that would disprove this statement."

Multiple Witnesses

There are multiple witnesses of Christ's resurrection that testify that He is alive. Jesus appeared to Mary Magdalene at the tomb. He appeared to the women who had come to anoint His body when they were on their way from the tomb. He appeared to two disciples on the Emmaus Road. He appeared to 10 of the 11 disciples in the upper room on Sunday night and again to Thomas and the disciples. He appeared to 500 believers gathered together on the hillsides of Galilee before His ascension into heaven. They reported that He appeared to them during a period of 40 days. Paul the apostle recounted that Jesus appeared to more than 500 of His followers at one time, the majority of whom were still alive and who could confirm what Paul wrote.

The Resurrection's Life-changing Truths

The Bible often clothes profound lessons in simple terms. Matthew's Gospel simply states, "Now after the Sabbath, as the first day of the week began to dawn, Mary Magdalene and the other Mary came to see the tomb" (Matthew 28:1).

We pause for a moment to reflect on the significance of this passage. Think about the disciples' thoughts that Sabbath. They were disappointed, discouraged, and downhearted. Their hopes had danced away like a shadow. Peter and John had left their prosperous fishing business to follow him. They had risked their future and their fortune on this itinerant Jewish preacher from Nazareth. But what now? What was their future? Jesus was dead.

Matthew had risked his entire career to follow Jesus. He had a secure position as a tax collector. He couldn't go back to his previous employment now, with all the ridicule he had experienced. His career as a tax collector was over. What did his future look like during the hours of Friday night and Sabbath?

And think about Mary, this woman from Magdala. She was a woman of ill repute who had found forgiveness, mercy, and grace in Christ. For the first time in her life she had discovered One who loved her with a pure, unselfish, divine love. He had cast the demons out of her life that had tormented her for so long. In Him she had found a new hope. In Him she had discovered a reason for living. In Him she had new purpose. In Him she had a future today, tomorrow, and forever.

But now He was dead. The last time she had seen His body, it was broken, bruised, and bloody. She had turned away in anguish and deep sorrow at His crucifixion. She could not bear seeing the thick red blood spurting from His hands or His blood-tinged face. She could not bear looking at the sorrow in His eyes or His pain-racked body. She could not bear the horror of it all.

Let's join Mary and her companions as they are on their way to the tomb to embalm the body of Christ. It is sunrise. The darkness is fading away. The past few days have been days of deep sorrow and disappointment. Their hopes have been dashed like a bottle thrown against the wall and broken into a thousand pieces. The disciples were sequestered in the upper room, fearing to leave, uncertain of their future. During the COVID-19 pandemic, millions of people were bound to their homes in a sort of self-quarantine, absolutely petrified to leave.

Consider Mary as she approached the tomb. The death of Christ had dashed their hopes and shattered their dreams. What thoughts must have been going through her mind? She must have wondered how to make sense out of the events of the past few days. She must have been confused, perplexed, and stunned by what had happened during the past 48 hours, but nevertheless she stepped out in faith to embalm His body.

The women did not have all their questions answered. They were confused about many of the events that had taken place that weekend and certainly had no idea how they would move the huge stone that sealed the tomb. The Roman guards certainly would never break the Roman seal on the tomb and open it for them. They had no idea how the problem would be solved, but this they knew: they had a duty to do, and they would leave the rest with God. You do not have to have all the answers to do what God places in your heart to do.

Faith does not mean you see; it means you trust. Faith is not knowing; it is believing. Faith is not having all the answers; it is having confidence that God still loves me and is working things out for my best when I do not understand. Remember the first verse in Matthew 28? "Now after the Sabbath, as the first day of the week began to dawn." Here is an eternal truth. After the darkness the sun always rises. Night turns into day. In your hour of deepest darkness, Jesus, the Sun of righteousness, will rise in your life. You do not need to understand. Only believe. Believe He cares. Believe He loves you. Believe He has the best in mind for you. Believe that in the light of the resurrected Christ, the Sun will rise again for you. He is the light of the world and will chase the darkness away.

There is a strange twist in the Resurrection story. We find it in John 20:11-17. "But Mary stood outside by the tomb weeping." Two angels ask, "Why are you weeping?" She responds, "because they have taken away my Lord, and I do not know where [to find Him]." While she was saying this, she turns and sees Jesus, but doesn't recognize Him. There are many people who feel that they do not know where or how to find Jesus. The interesting thing is this: Mary was looking for Jesus, and He was standing right beside her. Her experience reminds us of God's promise in Hebrews 13:5, "I will never leave you nor forsake you," and the promise in Isaiah 41:10, "Fear not, for I am with you; be not dismayed, for I am your God. I will strengthen you, yes, I will help you, I will uphold you with My righteous right hand."

Through her tears she did not see Him, but He was there. Where is Christ when it seems you cannot find Him? Where is Jesus when your spiritual life has dried up and you wonder where He has gone? He is right there by your side to strengthen you, to encourage you, and to give you hope. It does seem a little strange, though, that Jesus did not first appear to Peter, James, John, or Matthew. Why did Jesus appear to Mary? Mary had the greatest need. Jesus is with us always, but in times of our greatest need He is preciously near. Here is the first life-changing lesson of the Resurrection story: Rejoice! Christ is risen! Morning has come. Darkness is gone. Hope has dawned.

There is a second eternal truth we cannot miss. The tomb is empty. Death has lost. Life has won. Satan could not keep Jesus in the ground. Christ's resurrection points us to the day that Jesus will come, and our dead loved ones will be resurrected too. You may have recently lost a loved one. Like Mary, your eyes are filled with tears, your heart is broken, your grief is deep, but resurrection morning speaks hope. It speaks courage. It speaks of new life. Jesus has the antidote for the virus of sin. He died for us. He lives for us. He is coming again for us.

Every time Jesus confronted death in the New Testament, death lost, and Jesus won. Jesus faced death head-on at Jairus', the ruler of the synagogue's, home. When he spoke the words "Little girl, I say to you, arise," death fled away (Mark 5:41). Death loses its stranglehold in the presence of the living Christ. Again at the tomb of Lazarus, in the presence of the resurrected Christ, death lost, and Jesus won. The grave could not hold Jesus' friend when the Master declared, "Lazarus, come forth." Death was defeated, and Lazarus came out of the tomb alive (John 11:43). And at the tomb of Christ that Resurrection morning, death was defeated.

At the tomb of Christ that Resurrection morning, the last enemy was overcome. At the tomb of Christ that Resurrection morning, Satan's greatest weapon was demolished. Death was defeated. Now our hearts can beat with hope. The words of the apostle Paul come echoing down the corridors of time: "Behold, I tell you a mystery: We shall not all sleep, but we shall all be changed—in a moment, in the twinkling of an eye, at the last trumpet. For the trumpet will sound, and the dead will be raised incorruptible, and we shall be changed" (1 Corinthians 15:51, 52). Jesus' resurrection is the eternal guarantee that those who have believed in Him and have been changed by His grace will one day be resurrected when He returns to take us home.

At the tomb of Christ that Resurrection morning, our eternal destiny was sealed, for without the Resurrection, the eternal life Christ promised could not be realized. This is the very reason the New Testament writers place such repeated emphasis on the Resurrection. They mention it hundreds of times. On that Resurrection morning 2,000 years ago Christ triumphed over Satan. Life triumphed over death. Faith triumphed over fear. Hope triumphed over despair. Joy triumphed over sorrow. It is time to rejoice. Christ has risen. Death has lost its hold on us, and one day soon Jesus is coming to take us home.

CHAPTER 4

THRIVING IN LIFE'S TOUGHEST TIMES

Recently the world has experienced a life-threatening pandemic termed COVID-19. More than 2.5 million people were infected, with hundreds of thousands of deaths. During this time one of the greatest needs of medical professionals was personal protective equipment, or PPE.

PPE refers to protective clothing, helmets, gloves, face shields, goggles, face masks, respirators, and other equipment designed to protect medical professionals from exposure to infection or illness. Because COVID-19 is airborne, it was crucial for medical professionals to have the necessary protective equipment. During the crisis there was a shortage of PPE in some areas, so many health-care workers contracted COVID-19. Although these medical personel were extremely busy serving others, they were not immune from the virus. They needed PPE to survive.

Another Deadly Pandemic

There is another deadly pandemic with a virus that is even more fatal than the coronavirus. Sin's virus has infected the entire human family, and we are on the front lines of the battle. Each one of us during sin's pandemic also need PPE. If in our busyness we neglect our personal protective equipment, we are likely to be infected with the virus of sin. If in our frantic rush through life we do not take time to care for the spiritual part of our nature, we may contract a fatal spiritual disease.

The Apostle Paul's Counsel

The apostle Paul wrote, "For we do not wrestle against flesh and blood, but against principalities, against powers, against the rulers of the darkness of this age, against spiritual hosts of wickedness in the heavenly places. Therefore take up the whole armor of God, that you may be able to withstand in the evil day, and having done all, to stand" (Ephesians 6:12, 13). The armor of God is our PPE against the virus of sin. When medical professionals entered a coronavirus patient's room, they would not think of entering without some type of protective gear on. Every day we enter the evil one's territory, where millions are being infected by the virus of sin, and we are not immune. To enter unprotected is spiritual disaster. With God's armor on, we can thrive in life's toughest times. It is His protective equipment in times of trial.

What is this protective equipment divinely given to us by God in this conflict between good and evil? The apostle Paul gives us a hint in 2 Corinthians 10:4: "For the weapons of our warfare are not carnal but mighty in God for pulling down strongholds." What are these weapons of God? How can we be prepared spiritually for the crises we face in our personal lives? What is the source of our spiritual strength? What resources has God given us to fight the virus of sin? One of God's choice weapons is His Word. "The word of God is living and powerful, and sharper than any two-edged sword, piercing even to the division of soul and spirit, and of joints and marrow, and is a discerner of the thoughts and intents of the heart" (Hebrews 4:12). The Bible is the living Word of God. Through the ministry of the Holy Spirit it becomes alive in our hearts and changes our lives. Other books may be inspiring, but God's Word is inspired. Other books may enlighten the mind, but God's Word not only enlightens us, it transforms us.

God's Word: A Creative Word

The inspired Word of God contains life changing principles. The creative power of the Word of God illuminates our darkness. It changes us. When God spoke the word at Creation, our planet came into existence. He created this world by His all-powerful Word. The psalmist states, "By the word of the Lord the heavens were made, and all the host of them by the breath of His mouth. . . . For He spoke, and it was done; He commanded, and it stood fast" (Psalm 33:6-9).

God's word is a creative word. What He says is so, even if it were never so before, because His word is so powerful that it creates what it declares. The audible word proceeding out of God's mouth creates tangible matter. You and I can declare what is, but God can declare what is not, and what is not appears when God speaks, because His word makes it so. Speaking about Abraham and Sarah's conception in old age, Paul states this remarkable truth: "God . . . calls those things which do not exist as though they did" (Romans 4:17). Before Sarah ever conceived a child, God's word had declared that she would become pregnant in old age. This divine pronouncement became a reality, because God's word has the power to accomplish what God declares.

Here is a marvelous, life-changing truth: the creative power of the spoken word is in the written Word. The power of the Word brings light into darkened minds. The power of the Word quenches thirsty souls and feeds hungry hearts. It re-creates the soul in the image of God. It strengthens us in the battle between good and evil. When Jesus was tempted in the wilderness, He met Satan head-on with these words: "It is written, 'Man shall not live by bread alone, but by every word that proceeds from the mouth of God'" (Matthew 4:4). The ancient Scriptures, the Holy Bible, nourishes our souls. Its teachings satisfy our deepest longings. Just as the body is sustained, satisfied, and strengthened by healthy, nourishing food, our souls are sustained, strengthened, and satisfied by the Word of God. But this leads us to another vital question: Is the Bible merely an inspiring book, like many others, or is it truly a divinely inspired book given to us by God? If the Bible is God's divine revelation to humanity, then we neglect its teachings at the peril of eternal loss. If the Bible is simply an inspiring human document, then it has little power to radically transform us. So the question of the Bible's inspiration is critically important. In fact, it may be a matter of life and death. Let's examine the evidence.

The Inspiration of the Bible

The blazing Palestinian sun beat mercilessly down on a young Arab boy herding his few sheep in a remote area by the Dead Sea. It was just another ordinary day in his life. Each morning he led the sheep in search of a few morsels of food across the burning desert sands. He had no idea that this day would change the world.

When one of his sheep wandered away into a cave, he attempted to scare it out by throwing a stone into the cave. To his surprise, he heard the breaking of pottery. Thinking he had discovered some valuable hidden treasure, he raced home to tell his father. What they discovered in the cave that day was far more valuable than some ancient noblemen's riches. There on the shores of the Dead Sea in 1947 the Dead Sea Scrolls were discovered. The clay jars in the cave held a valuable treasure. They contained the oldest Bible manuscripts in existence. These scrolls were written by the Qumran community approximately 150 years before Christ. These people were called the Essenes. They spent hours hand copying the Bible. To ensure accuracy, their copying laws were extremely strict. Some of the world's most outstanding Bible scholars and specialists in ancient biblical languages have pored over these manuscripts for decades. These ancient scrolls eloquently testify to the accuracy and reliability of the Bible. In addition to the Dead Sea Scrolls there are numerous other copies of the Old Testament from the early centuries and beyond. When all these manuscripts are compared, there is a remarkable harmony testifying to the accuracy of the transmission. In addition to the Old Testament manuscript copies there are more than 2,400 New Testament manuscripts from the first to fourth centuries. The Bible has been copied and recopied more than any single book in the world. The accuracy of these copies testifies to the Bible's divine inspiration.

From Generation to Generation

Down through the millenniums God's Word has been accurately passed from one generation to the next. From the Bible's first book, Genesis, to its last, Revelation, it answers our deepest questions and speaks to our heart's deepest needs. The Bible was written during a 1,500-year span by more than 40 authors. Many of these authors did not know one another. They lived in different places, spoke different languages, and were products of different cultures, yet each one writing under the inspiration of the Holy Spirit presents God's eternal plan for the human race clearly. There is no contradiction on these main themes of Scripture. There is an amazing unity of thought and purpose throughout the Bible. The Scriptures reflect the thoughts of a divine mind. In 3,000 places the Bible writers declare "and God said," "and the Lord spoke," or phrases similar. The Bible writers believed they were inspired by God, and the evidence within Scripture reveals that the messages are of divine origin.

The fulfillment of numerous biblical prophecies reveals the truthfulness of Scripture. There are approximately 31,000 verses in the Bible, and a little more than 8,000 of these—more than 25 percent—

contain prophecy. These prophecies are amazingly accurate, revealing the names of nations and world rulers. They reveal minute details of the life of Christ in advance. Here are just a few examples. Christ's biography was written hundreds of years in advance. Jesus hometown, of course, was Nazareth, but 700 years in advance, the prophet Micah predicted the Messiah would be born in Bethlehem (see Micah 5:2). A decree of Caesar Augustus brought Mary and Joseph to Bethlehem the exact night of Christ's birth. This is remarkable. Nazareth is a city in Galilee, in the north of Israel. Bethlehem is about 90 miles to the south, in Judea. This is just one of the amazing prophecies relating to Jesus' birth, life, death, and resurrection. The book of Numbers, written 1,500 years in advance, predicted that a star would rise in the east as a sign of the Messiah's birth (see Numbers 24:17). Christ's ministry is described in detail in Isaiah 61:1-3. His death, including His crucifixion, is outlined in Psalm 22 about 1,000 years before it happened. Remarkably enough, even the betrayal price of 30 pieces of silver is foretold by Zechariah centuries before it occurred (see Zechariah 11:11, 12).

The Old Testament prophecies reveal the rise and fall of nations, the destiny of kings and rulers, and the future of our world with minute accuracy. The prophet Daniel predicts the rise of the four great nations that would dominate the Middle East and rule the then-known world in Babylon, Media-Persia, Greece, and Rome, including the breakup of the Roman Empire (see Daniel 2; 7; 8). In Matthew 24 Jesus gives startling predictions of the last days that are now being fulfilled. These are just a few of the prophecies that clearly demonstrate the reliability, truthfulness, and divine origin of the Holy Word of God.

The Bible's Main Purpose

The main purpose of the Bible is to unfold God's eternal plan of salvation. The Bible contains history, but it is not primarily a history book. The Bible touches on science, but it is not a scientific textbook. The Bible provides insights into the human mind, but it is not a treatise on psychology. Although God's Word touches on a variety of disciplines, it is first and foremost a revelation of God's will, revealing God's eternal truths to humanity. The Bible answers the three great questions of life: "Why am I here?" "Where did I come from?" and "What does the future hold?" It provides hope and courage for each and every one of us.

The central theme of the Bible is Jesus. The prophets of the Old Testament testified of Him. Each book of the Bible is a revelation of His love. Speaking to the Pharisees, Jesus declared, "You search the Scriptures, for in them you think you have eternal life; and these are they which testify of Me" (John 5:39). The Old Testament speaks of the Christ who will come, and the New Testament reveals the Christ who has come. All the Bible "testifies" of Jesus. In Scripture Jesus is the dying lamb, the living priest, and the coming king. He is the one who justifies us, sanctifies us, and one day will glorify us. Jesus is our forgiving, merciful, compassionate, life-changing Savior and Lord.

Jesus is the great miracle worker. He is the life changer. Jesus added, "The words that I speak to you are spirit, and they are life" (John 6:63). The Holy Spirit takes the principles of God's Word, impresses them in receptive minds, and makes us new. Christ is at the center of all scriptural teaching, and so, as the apostle Paul states so clearly, "if anyone is in Christ, he is a new creation; old things have passed away; behold, all things have become new" (2 Corinthians 5:17).

The Bible is not merely a to-do manual on how to construct a Christian life. Consider some of the scriptural symbols of the Word, including light, fire, a hammer, seed, and bread. These varied images have one thing in common: they reveal the power of God's Word to change our lives. The Word of God is like a light that guides us through the dark valleys of our lives. It is like a fire that burns within our souls. It is like a hammer that breaks our hard hearts. It is like seed that silently grows and produces the fruits of the Spirit in our lives. It is like bread that nourishes our spiritual hunger.

Symbols of God's Word

The psalmist David declares, "Your word is a lamp to my feet and a light to my path" (Psalm 119:105). He also adds, "The entrance of Your words gives light; it gives understanding to the simple" (verse 130). Light always involves the removal of darkness. If you were on a dark path at night without a light, you may easily get off the path. It would not be uncommon to stumble and fall into a deep ravine without a light. A powerful flashlight would make all the difference. The Word of God lights the pathway of the followers of Christ. It guides us home. Jesus is the "light of the world" who lights up our darkness through His Word (John 8:12). When we share the Word of God with others, it dispels the darkness that Satan has enshrouded their lives with, and lightens their pathway to the kingdom of God. My wife and I live about a mile from our Living Hope Seventh-day Adventist Church. Often after an evening program we will walk home. Our journey home takes us through a tree-lined path through the woods that is not lighted. We have walked that path in almost total darkness at times, and it is difficult to keep on the path and find our way. We have learned by experience that having a flashlight makes all the difference. When the light illumines the path, the walk home is quite pleasant. Without the light, we are groping in the darkness. Jesus longs to get us home, so He has provided His Word as a lamp to light the way.

In Jeremiah 23:29 God's Word is compared to both a fire and a hammer. It is compared to a fire because it consumes. When we read the Word of God, the fire of God's Word burns within us, consuming error. Like gold refined in the fire, the dross is consumed. The refining process is not always pleasant, but it is necessary to remove the dross in our characters. God's Word is also like a hammer. The term *hammer* may seem to be a rare term to use to describe the Bible. Hammers nail things together. They also smash things. The hammer of God's Word smashes hard hearts to pieces. Think of the dramatic changes that took place in the lives of the demoniacs, the Roman centurion, the thief on the cross, and a host of others throughout the New Testament. The Word of God pounded away at their hard hearts until they were broken by the hammer of love.

In one of the more common symbols in Scripture, the Bible is compared to "seed." In Luke 8:11 Jesus states, "The seed is the word of God." There is life in a tiny seed. When the seed of God's Word is planted in the soil of the mind, it produces an abundant harvest in the life. Jesus often used the symbolism of seed to describe the growth of His kingdom. The Word of God scattered like seed throughout the world will produce a bountiful harvest. Jesus expands on this theme in one of His farming parables. "And He said, 'The kingdom of God is as if a man should scatter seed on the ground, and should sleep by night and rise by day, and the seed should sprout and grow, he himself does not know how' " (Mark 4:26, 27). The Word of God may seem buried someplace within the mind. It may seem to be covered under the clods of sin, but if it is cherished, it will spring forth into new life. It will radically change our attitudes, our conversation, our habits, and our lifestyle. Seed is life-giving. We may not see the seed growing, but it is growing in our minds to produce its life-giving results.

The Bible also uses the term *bread* to describe the Word of God. Jesus said, "I am the bread of life" (John 6:35). He adds, "Man shall not live by bread alone, but by every word that proceeds from the mouth of God" (Matthew 4:4). Bread is the staff of life throughout the ancient world and one of our planet's basic foods. It is an essential dietary item. An individual can survive a long time on only bread and water. By using the illustration of bread, Jesus is declaring that He is essential for life.

In His well-known bread-of-life sermon (following the miracle of the feeding of 5,000) Jesus declares, "Whoever eats My flesh and drinks My blood has eternal life" (John 6:54). This seems to be a very strange statement. What could Jesus possibly be talking about? Obviously He was not talking about literally eating His flesh and drinking His blood. By feasting on His Word, His teachings become a very part of our lives. This is what Jeremiah meant when he joyfully declared, "Your words were found, and I ate them, and Your word was to me the joy and rejoicing of my heart; for I am called by Your name, O Lord God of hosts" (Jeremiah 15:16). The Word of God, like a good piece of whole-wheat bread, satisfies our hidden hunger. Have you ever noticed that highly refined products are neither satisfying nor filling? The Word of God is the staff of life. It nourishes our souls. And of course, the Scriptures are like a cool draft of refreshing pure water. They completely satisfy. There is nothing as rewarding as the discovery of the truth about Jesus in every teaching of Scripture. When we discover these wonderful truths about Jesus, we are blessed beyond measure.

The Indestructibility of the Bible

Infidels have tried to destroy credibility in the Bible for centuries. Their goal is to use sophisticated arguments to erode faith in God's

Word, yet the Bible remains the best seller of all time. Each year more than 100 million copies of the Bible are sold or given away free. *Guinness World Records* estimates that more than 5 billion copies of the Bible have been printed in hundreds of languages. The French philosopher Voltaire, born in 1694, was a fierce critic of Christianity. He believed that the Bible was filled with "absurdities" and that society was living in the "twilight of Christianity." As a prolific writer he wrote 20,000 letters and 2,000 books. A significant portion of his writings were an attack on the Christian faith and the Bible. It is reported that near the end of his life he declared that his writings would displace the Bible. He believed that within 100 years the Scriptures would be a relic of the past and soon forgotten. Within 25 years of Voltaire's death (on May 30, 1778), the printing presses that had published his works were used for printing Bibles in the common language of the people.

There is another interesting aspect of this story. Daniel Merritt, Ph.D., Th.D., has done extensive research on Voltaire and reports that Henri Tronchin, who served as president of the Geneva Bible Society from 1834 to 1839, lived in Voltaire's former residence. When the Bibles were printed on the presses that previously had printed Voltaire's books, many of them were stored in Voltaire's home, then occupied by the president of the Geneva Bible Society less than 100 years later. What an amazing twist to the story. This reminds us of Jesus' statement in Matthew 24:35: "Heaven and earth will pass away, but My words will by no means pass away." Isaiah the prophet adds, "The grass withers, the flower fades, but the word of our God stands forever" (Isaiah 40:8). The Bible has been maligned, criticized, ridiculed, torn apart, and burned, yet it stands as a testimony to its divine authorship. It speaks of grace, mercy, forgiveness, and new life to every generation.

The Bible's Life-changing Power

The greatest testimony of the inspiration of the Bible is its ability through the power of the Holy Spirit to transform lives completely. Let me share with you Mr. Chen's story. Mr. Chen, as an ardent Communist, was an atheist. As far as he was concerned, all Christians were nothing more than ignorant, mindless, uneducated peasants.

Hope for Troubled Times

One day in 1992 Mr. Chen returned home on leave from his military service and discovered that his wife had become a Seventh-day Adventist Christian. From 1991 to1993 there was a Holy Spirit revival in northeastern China, and in one city, between 2,000 and 3,000 people were baptized each year. When Mr. Chen discovered that his wife was a Bible-believing Christian, he became furious. His anger boiled over. He yelled, threatened, and intimidated her.

Then his wife developed a serious eye infection that required surgery. He sat by her bed in the hospital for hours each day. As she began to recover, she started reading the Bible with her one good eye and a patch over the other eye. Her doctor suggested she rest both eyes, but she felt she needed strength from the Word of God. In desperation her husband said, "It's bad enough that I have a wife who is a Christian. I don't want a wife who is blind as well. Give me that book, and I will read to you."

She requested that he read the book of Job. The more he read, the more interested he became. He was amazed at Job's faith. He could not understand how someone going through such difficulties and facing such trials could trust God. When he came to the end of Job, he was further amazed when he read that God turned Job's tragedy into triumph: "And the Lord restored Job's losses when he prayed for his friends. Indeed the Lord gave Job twice as much as he had before. . . . Now the Lord blessed the latter days of Job more than his beginning" (Job 42:10-12).

Mr. Chen continued to secretly read the Bible when his wife was out of the room for her treatments. Soon he could resist no longer, and there in that hospital room he surrendered to the claims of Christ. Today he is a Christian pastor, powerfully preaching the Word of God and cherishing the Bible he once despised. The life-changing truths of God's Word made all the difference for Mr. Chen.

The Bible speaks to people of all cultures, backgrounds, and languages. It presents hope in troubled times for all peoples. Heaven's call is to spend time with God's Word. Let the beauty of Scripture bathe your soul. Find that quiet spot and allow the Holy Spirit to move in your life. Sense anew the power of the Word of God. It changed Mr. Chen's life, and it can change yours, too.

CHAPTER 5

STAYING HEALTHY IN A SICK WORLD

Sickness not only is debilitating to the body but also plays havoc with our minds. When we are sick, it is much easier to become discouraged or even depressed. Have you ever been sick for a week? How do you feel at the end of the week? What about two weeks? During the COVID-19 pandemic those infected with the disease reported overwhelming physical symptoms, including a raging fever followed by the chills, intense muscle pain, a persistent cough, shortness of breath, a sore throat, violent headaches, and fatigue. One victim said, "I felt like I was drowning," and another added, "Nights were horrible. My temperature would rise. My body would burn with fever, and then suddenly I would shake with the chills. But worst of all, I felt so alone in isolation." One of the great consequences of this pandemic was that the virus was so contagious that individuals often had to suffer through their illness alone. Their loved ones had a very difficult time giving them the care they needed.

Tragically some people even died in lonely hospital rooms, isolated from their families. It is incredibly difficult to suffer in the advanced stages of the coronavirus for two weeks, but what if you were sick for 12 years? What if you were in constant pain, considered an outcast separated from your family year after year? Mark's Gospel records the story of a woman who suffered for 12 long years.

"Now a certain woman had a flow of blood for twelve years" (Mark 5:25). She hemorrhaged continually. Her clothes were stained with this continual stream of blood. She was tired, worn out, emaciated, and weak. But worst of all, she could no longer experience the warm embrace of others. She could no longer enjoy a child's hug or one jumping up on her lap. She was discouraged, depressed, and desperate. She wanted to be well. She longed for healing. She searched for a cure, but nothing seemed to work.

Mark's Gospel continues her story in these sorrowful words: "[She] had suffered many things from many physicians" (verse 26). The very ones who were supposed to help had only caused more harm. She had "suffered many things from many physicians." The cures they had offered had only made her worse. She had spent her hard-earned savings on their quack cures.

She was not only desperate but hopeless. She was not only discouraged but in total despair. Darkness filled her soul. She had spent her money on these so-called physicians, only to be worse off. Then she met the Master Physician, Jesus. A huge crowd surrounded the Savior. As He slowly made His way along the narrow, rocky roadway, the crowd pressed Him on every side. This poor woman wondered if she would ever get near enough to beg for healing. He had healed others. Would He heal her? Mark's Gospel reveals her desperation in these words: "If only I may touch His clothes, I shall be made well" (verse 28).

The Gospel of Luke also records this story and is even more precise. Luke was a physician and reveals some fascinating details in his Gospel. In Luke 8:43 he tells the story of this poor suffering woman, and he says, "[She] could not be healed by any" of the physicians. The word for healed used in this Bible passage has as its root the word "therapy." No therapy could be found for her. Nothing that she had tried had worked. Jesus was her last and only hope for help. If He could not help her, she was doomed to a life of constant pain and continual sickness. She pressed her way through the crowd, believing if she could only touch the hem of Christ's garment, she would be healed. She wanted something, anything, that would cure her disease. She had searched for it and spent her life savings to find that magic cure. Her response is the typical response of many a person today when they face some debilitating disease. They are desperate to find something, anything, that will cure the disease.

Every patient wants something to cure their illness, anything that will bring relief. They are desperate for a cure, whether it is a pill or some other type of medication to solve the problem. Modern medicine focuses on diagnosing and healing disease, but Jesus focuses on something more—much more. Finally she was able to stretch her hand between two people crowding around Jesus and briefly touch just the hem of His garment. In that touch was concentrated the faith of her life. The Master can distinguish the touch of faith from the press of the crowd. Healing power flowed into her body. The disease was gone. She was miraculously healed.

Then Jesus made a remarkable statement to this woman: "Daughter, be of good cheer; your faith has made you well" (verse 48). She is not some nameless face in the crowd. Not some human statistic. She is a child of God. Jesus calls her daughter. He encourages her with the words "Be of good cheer; your faith has made you well" (verse 48).

This word for "well" is used more than 100 times in the New Testament, and most of those times it is translated "salvation." Jesus declared this woman was whole again. Her faith grasped the reality of His divinity. In His loving mercy He revealed His grace to this desperate, hopeless woman and made her well again. Physically, mentally, emotionally, and spiritually she was made well. This is the work of Jesus. Our total health matters to Jesus because we matter to Jesus. He longs for us to live life to the fullest in this world of sickness, suffering, and death.

Restoration: The Goal of Jesus' Life

Jesus' goal is to restore, through the gospel, His image in humanity. This restoration includes physical, mental, emotional, and spiritual healing. In John 10:10 Jesus reveals His plan for each one of us: "The thief does not come except to steal, and to kill, and to destroy. I have come that they may have life, and that they may have it more abundantly." The devil wants to destroy our health, and Jesus wants to restore our health. The devil wants to discourage us, but Jesus wants to encourage us. The devil wants to tear us down, but Jesus wants to build us up. The devil wants us to be sick; Jesus wants us to be healthy. Jesus is interested in the whole person. He longs for us to be physically healthy, mentally alert, emotionally stable, and spiritually well. This is especially true in the light of His soon return. This world is facing an enormous crisis. Jesus' own predictions in Matthew 24 and Luke 21 foretell catastrophic conditions on the earth just before His return. These events will break upon this world as an overwhelming surprise for those who are unprepared. The apostle Paul underscores the necessity of total health in the light of eternity in these words: "Now may the God of peace Himself sanctify you completely; and may your whole spirit, soul, and body be preserved blameless at the coming of our Lord Jesus Christ" (1 Thessalonians 5:23). The word "spirit" here has to do with our attitude or emotions. Sometimes even today we might say, "She has a gentle spirit," or "He has an angry spirit." What are we talking about? The attitude or the emotional part of the person. The word "soul" in this passage is speaking about the spiritual nature. The part of our being that longs for God and eternity. The "body" in this passage is obviously our physical nature. Jesus longs for every aspect of our nature to be sanctified, or made holy, through the power of His Spirit. The apostle Paul emphasizes this thought again in his epistle to the Romans. "With eyes wide open to the mercies of God, I beg you, my brothers, as an act of **intelligent worship**, to give him your **bodies**, as a living sacrifice, consecrated to him and acceptable by him. Don't let the world around you squeeze you into its own mould, but let God re-make you so that your whole attitude of **mind** is changed. Thus you will prove in practice that the will of God's good, acceptable to him and perfect" (Romans 12:1, 2, Phillips; emphasis added). Did you notice the apostle's emphasis on the whole person? He speaks of our worship, our bodies, and our minds. Caring for our bodies is an act of intelligent worship. After all our Creator has made us, and as we care for our bodies, we are giving honor to our Creator.

At Creation God surrounded Adam and Eve with all the elements necessary for optimum health. Clear babbling brooks and flowing streams provided them with pure water. Fruits, nuts, grains, and some types of vegetables grew in abundance. The natural diet God provided was packed with wholesome nutrients. As our first parents exercised in the sunshine and fresh air, their bodies maintained the health God created them with. Evenings brought a refreshing mist, and each day they rested in His love and care. On the seventh day, Sabbath, they entered into an experience of deeper trust as they worshipped their Creator on the special day that He had sanctified, or set apart, for worship.

Our first parents lived in a world free of stress, anxiety, and disease. Peace and happiness walked through the land together. Their hearts were filled with love for God and for one another. It is God's intent that we discover principles from Eden to guide our lives today. Creation was not simply an act of God millenniums ago. It was a model for us in how to live today. God is not interested only in our spiritual health. He is interested in our physical and emotional health as well. There is a close relationship between our physical and spiritual well-being. The apostle John states it succinctly: "Beloved, I pray that you may prosper in all things and be in health, just as your soul prospers" (3 John 2).

Science Confirms We Are Whole Human Beings

During the past 25 years there has been a significant resurgence in the concept of whole person care. The World Health Organization that since 1948 had defined health as a state of complete physical, mental, and social well-being has now recognized the need for a fourth component, spirituality, to be considered as an important element of health. Since 2010 there have been more than 2,000 studies on the impact of religion and health. A growing body of scientific evidence confirms the accuracy of the Bible's teaching on health. Degenerative diseases, as the result of faulty living habits, are rapidly rising. Heart disease, strokes, and cancer top the list of killer diseases taking the lives of people prematurely. What do the majority of these scientific studies on health indicate? Where does the research point? Here are three specific areas where faith can make a dramatic difference in your health.

1. Faith leads people to make better health choices.

Fewer people who are religious and have a deep commitment to God smoke, abuse alcohol, or use harmful drugs. They exercise more, eat more healthfully, and guard their rest. When people believe that they were created by God and their bodies are the temple of His Spirit, their health choices are more positive. They are guided by the apostle Paul's words in 1 Corinthians 10:31: "Therefore, whether you eat or drink, or whatever you do, do all to the glory of God." People of faith become more conscious of their health and choose to live more healthfully.

You may wonder what some of those health choices are and how can you improve your health. Recently Harvard University conducted a massive study to determine what health habits could keep people living longer. This is what they discovered: by maintaining five health habits, you may be able to add as many as 10 years to your life. Here are the simple habits that will increase your life expectancy: eating a healthy diet, exercising regularly, keeping a healthy body weight, not drinking too much alcohol, and not smoking. Maintaining these habits during adulthood may add more than a decade to life expectancy, according to a new study led by the Harvard T. H. Chan School of Public Health (Harvard University study, April 2019). Researchers also found that American women and men who maintained the healthiest lifestyles were 82 percent less likely to die from cardiovascular disease and 65 percent less likely to die from cancer when compared with those with the least-healthy lifestyles over the course of the roughly 30-year study period.

Let's look at these health builders a little more carefully. One of the very critical issues with COVID-19—and all other diseases, for that matter—is strengthening our immune systems. The immune system is a complex network of cells and proteins that defends our bodies against infections and disease. If you build a strong immune system, not only do you reduce the risk of getting sick, but if you do get sick, the symptoms will tend to be much less, and the duration of your illness shorter. There is no guarantee that any one of us will not get sick. However, there are certainly ways we can protect ourselves and build our immunity.

   a. Eat Healthy: Nutrition is key in any illness both as prevention and assisting in the cure. Fruits and vegetables, as well as whole grains, reduce inflammation and improve blood vessel function. Plant foods are loaded with health-promoting, protective phytochemicals that neutralize the oxidative stress of infections and other diseases. They reduce inflammation and enhance the health of the blood vessel lining to assure needed blood supply. Animal protein has inflammatory substances that break down the bodies' immune system. Plant foods, including beans, legumes, salads, and vegetables, provide the building blocks to produce the substances that make blood vessels work well. We also suggest a rainbow of colors on your plate, assuring that all the protective nutrients are included in your diet both as prevention and as adjunct to cure if you do get sick. Of course, avoiding sugar is a must, as sugar impairs white blood cell function, which is vital in fighting off foreign substances in our bodies.

b. Drink Lots of Water: Water protects the body from dehydration, allowing every cell to function and fight at peak performance. Therefore, it is a key element to enhancing our immune system. So drink lots of water! How much? At least eight (eight-ounce) glasses a day. Another way to monitor if you are getting enough is to drink enough so that you have at least one clear urination per day. Make sure to consume adequate water before 6:00 p.m. so that your sleep is not interrupted and vital rest compromised.

c. Get Adequate Fresh Air and Exercise: The issue of exercise is also important, and we recommend that whenever possible it be out in the outdoors. People who walk briskly at least five times a week for a minimum of 30 minutes per day have better health and live longer than those who do not exercise. Exercise is profoundly helpful in warding off disease. Each day, get out in the fresh air, breathe deeply, and walk with your head erect and your shoulders back. If you live in a city environment, look for a park to walk in that has shrubs and trees. It is unhealthful to breathe in the polluted air from the exhaust of vehicles in the traffic-jammed streets of our crowded cities. Trees and plants have life-giving properties that will build your health. Take deep, refreshing breaths in an outdoor natural setting in the sunshine. Sunshine is a natural source of vitamin D. When sunlight is absorbed in moderate amounts, so we do not burn, we are able to boost our immunity to disease by increasing our vitamin D. This can be done with as little as 15 minutes a day in the sunshine.

d. Get Plenty of Rest: One of the God-given principles of good health is rest. When we are ill, our bodies recover best when we rest. Even when we think we have recovered from an illness, it is best to be cautious and be sure to get extra rest for a few days. This is particularly important with COVID-19, because we don't know for sure when recovery occurs. Genetic material from the virus may be shed from the nostrils for up to four weeks. Rest is an important part of any good health plan. In fact, that's why once a week God has given us the seventh-day Sabbath as a day of rest from the stresses of life.

e. Avoid Tobacco, Alcohol, Harmful Drugs, and Stimulants: Cigarette smoking is the most preventable cause of death in the world. It contributes to hundreds of thousands of deaths each year. It is a major risk factor for heart disease, lung cancer, type 2 diabetes, and a host of other lifestyle diseases. It weakens the immune system, contributes to gum disease, heightens the risk of infertility, and is a cause of blood clots. Alcohol is a major contributor to premature death. It is a cause of some types of cancer, heart disease, and liver damage. Along with tobacco it is dangerously addictive. Excessive drinking leads to depression and numerous unintentional injuries, including car accidents. The conclusions of a recent British study, published in the renowned medical journal The Lancet, are "clear and unambiguous: alcohol is a colossal global health issue." The chief medical officer of the UK found that there is "no safe level of alcohol consumption."

One of the major problems with alcohol is that it affects the frontal lobes of the brain, where conscience, reason, and judgment are located. This impacts our decision-making process. The Holy Spirit communicates with our frontal lobes, leading us to make positive lifestyle decisions, to understand God's Word more fully, and to follow His truth more completely. Alcohol hinders that process and makes us less sensitive to God's revealed will.

Although we may not be able to avoid getting sick, we can put our immune systems in the best possible position to fight disease. We can strengthen our immune systems to combat illness.

2. Faith leads people to be more optimistic and positive.

This positive attitude helps them to reduce stress and hypertension. They are more at peace and have calmer dispositions. The University of Rochester's medical newsletter reports, "The idea of optimism leading to better health has been studied. Researchers have reviewed the results of over 80 studies to look for common findings. They found optimism had a remarkable impact on physical health. The study examined overall longevity, survival from a disease, heart health, immunity, cancer outcomes, pregnancy outcomes, pain tolerance, and other health topics. It seemed that those who had a more optimistic outlook did better and had better results than those who were pessimistic. The message is that having a positive attitude can boost your physical health, no matter what might be ailing you."

Faith leads to a deep trust in God, and that trust in God leads you to be much more optimistic and positive about life because you know God cares for you and is always seeking your best. This sense of God's presence in your life is both physically and emotionally healing.

3. Faith leads people to attend church more. The greater support system and sense of community contributes to greater well-being.

The University of California, Berkeley, reported in 2002 the results of a 31-year study of more than 6,500 adults in Alameda, California. The comprehensive report noted, "People who attend religious services have significantly lower risks of death compared with those who never attend or attend less frequently even if you adjust for age, health behaviors, and other risk factors."

Churchgoers live up to seven years longer than nonattendees, a University of Texas study has found. Researchers found that life expectancy rose when the number of church services attended increased. Those who attended every week had a life expectancy of 82 years. This dropped to 79 years for those who attended less than once a week, and for nonattendees it dropped to about 75 years (*The Sunday Mail*, September 26, 1999, p. 55).

God's Word reinforces the information in these studies. In Hebrews 10:23-25 the Bible shares this positive benefit of church attendance. "Let us hold fast the confession of our hope without wavering, for He who promised is faithful. And let us consider one another in order to stir up love and good works, not forsaking the assembling of ourselves together, as is the manner of some, but exhorting one another, and so much the more as you see the Day approaching."

Let's briefly analyze this divine counsel and compare it to the research we have been investigating. Our Bible passage encourages Christians to "assemble together" and

1. "Consider one another." In other words, attempt to understand the life circumstances of one another. Enter into one another's feelings. As the apostle Paul puts it in Galatians: "Bear one another's burdens, and so fulfill the law of Christ" (Galatians 6:2). Someone has said, "Anyone wrapped up in themselves is a very small package." And it is true. A community of faith enables us to relate on a level of unselfish concern for one another. This attitude of consideration for one another is healthful for the one who shares his life with another and for the one who receives the selfless sharing.

2. "Stir up love." Or motivate, inspire, lift one another up. Meeting together in worship, studying God's Word together, and praying together provides an opportunity to motivate one another and lift one another up.

3. "Encourage one another." There is nothing like an encouraging word to lift someone's spirits. Church above all should be a place of encouragement and hope. How do you feel when someone compliments you? It cheers you up and brings joy to your life. These positive healthy thoughts are life-giving.

How to Make Positive Changes

You may be wondering, *How can I make positive changes in my life? Where can I find the strength to put into practice good health practices? I have tried before and failed.* The key to change is uniting our weak wills with Christ's all-powerful strength. We may be weak, but He is strong. We may be frail, but He is almighty. On our own we cannot, but with Him we can. It all begins with our personal choice. All change begins with choice. The more we make excuses for our behavior, the more we will create a barrier to success. A remarkable experiment done by a marine biologist illustrates this point. During a research experiment a marine biologist placed a shark into a large holding tank, and then released several small bait fish into the tank. As you would expect, the shark quickly swam around the tank, and attacked and ate the smaller fish.

The marine biologist then inserted a strong piece of clear fiberglass into the tank, creating two separate partitions. She then put the shark on one side of the fiberglass and a new set of bait fish on the other.

Again, the shark quickly attacked. This time, however, the shark slammed into the fiberglass divider and bounced off. Undeterred, the shark kept repeating this behavior every few minutes, to no avail. Meanwhile, the bait fish swam around unharmed in the second partition. Eventually, about an hour into the experiment the shark gave up. This experiment was repeated several dozen times over the next few weeks. Each time the shark got less aggressive and made fewer attempts to attack the bait fish, until eventually the shark got tired of hitting the fiberglass divider and simply stopped attacking altogether.

The marine biologist then removed the fiberglass divider, but the shark didn't attack. The shark was trained to believe a barrier existed between it and the bait fish, so the bait fish swam wherever they wished, free from harm. Many of us, after experiencing setbacks and failures, emotionally give up and stop trying. Like the shark in the story, we believe that because we were unsuccessful in the past, we will always be unsuccessful. In other words, we continue to see a barrier in our heads, even when no "real" barrier exists between where we are and where we want to go.

When we make a choice to change, Christ immediately comes to our aid to break down the barriers and give us the strength we need. Our excuses keep us from receiving His power. At times we erect barriers in our minds. We think of all the reasons change is so difficult. We see the impossibilities, but God is the God of possibilities. He is the God who can make a way when we see no way. He is the God of the impossible making the impossible possible. The apostle Paul prays this prayer in Ephesians 3:20, 21: "Now to Him who is able to do exceedingly abundantly above all that we ask or think, according to the power that works in us, to Him be glory in the church by Christ Jesus to all generations, forever and ever. Amen." What can God do? He can do "exceedingly abundantly above all that we ask or think."

We may not understand how change takes place, but this we know: **God is able**.

Our minds may not be able to comprehend how He can make us into a new person, but this we know: **God is able**.

Our hearts may not be able to grasp how He can strengthen our weak wills, but this we know: **God is able**.

It may not seem possible, but God is able.

It may not seem logical, but God is able.

It may not seem likely, but God is able.

When under the promptings of the Holy Spirit we choose to make choices to live in harmony with the Creator's laws and give glory to Him in our lifestyle, He gives us the power to accomplish our desires. Our Creator creates within us the new life we have chosen to live as we commit ourselves to Him.

CHAPTER 6

THE DAY AFTER
THE DAY AFTER

As the world races through the twenty-first century, have you ever considered what our greatest need is? What do men and women living in the twenty-first century need most? If you were starving, it might be food. If you were homeless, it might be a place to live. If disease ravaged your body, it might be medicine. If you were lonely and discouraged, it might be love. Is there one thing more than any other that could take you through any difficulty you might face in life? Is there one thing that can make the human spirit soar? All over the world people are desperately looking for hope. Someone has well said, "What oxygen is to the lungs, hope is to the human spirit."

Hope buoys up our spirits. It lifts our vision from what is to what will be. It is a candle in the darkness. It provides encouragement for the future. Hope is one thing that lifts the human spirit and keeps us going amid the challenges we face. What is hope? How can we define it? Hope is that intangible quality that looks beyond life's difficulties to a better tomorrow. It leads us to live purposeful lives today because we know a new day is coming. It anticipates the best in life, even when we are facing the worst in life. It looks beyond what is to what will be. It keeps believing, trusting, anticipating, and expecting that out of today's darkness, tomorrow's light will shine more brightly.

The Roman statesman Pliny the Elder once said, "Hope is the pillar that holds up the world." He was right. Without hope, this world is on a collision course to disaster. Without hope, the foundations of society collapse. Without hope, we live our lives in silent despair.

Recently I read a story that was published in July 1991 in a little inspirational booklet titled *Bits and Pieces*. The story of a little boy who had been hospitalized after being badly burned illustrates the power of hope. The school system in a large city developed a program to help children keep up with their schoolwork if they needed to spend extensive time in the hospital. One of the special education teachers who was assigned to the program received a routine call asking her to visit a child. She took down the child's name and room number and talked briefly with the child's regular class teacher. "We're studying nouns and adverbs in his class now," the regular teacher said, "and I'd be grateful if you could help him understand them so he doesn't fall too far behind."

The hospital program teacher went to see the boy that afternoon. No one had mentioned to her that the boy had been badly burned and was in great pain. Upset at the sight of the boy, she stammered as she told him, "I've been sent by your school to help you with nouns and adverbs." When she left, she felt she had not accomplished very much at all.

But the next day a nurse asked her, "What did you do to that boy?" The teacher felt she must have done something wrong, and began to apologize. "No, no," said the nurse. "You don't know what I mean. We've been worried about that little boy, but ever since yesterday, his whole attitude has changed. He's fighting back, responding to treatment. It's as though he's decided to live."

Two weeks later the boy explained that he had completely given up hope until the teacher arrived. Everything changed when he came to a simple realization. He expressed it this way: "They wouldn't send a teacher to work on nouns and adverbs with a dying boy, would they?" What this badly burned child needed more than anything else was hope. Hope powerfully motivates us to look for the day after tomorrow. It paints the future in bright colors rather than dark shadows.

Rediscovering Hope

In a world that seems out of control, how can we rediscover hope? In a world that seems so uncertain, how can we hope again? In a world devastated by tsunamis, earthquakes, tornadoes, hurricanes, pestilences, and pandemics, is there something certain we can base our hope on? For example, the recent coronavirus pandemic has had catastrophic consequences. People all over the world have been infected. Hundreds of thousands have died. The world economy has been shattered. Unemployment rates have skyrocketed. Our lives have been changed forever. Where can we find hope? How can we look beyond our present trials to a brighter future the day after tomorrow?

Millions have found hope, assurance, and peace in a personal knowledge of and relationship with God through studying His Word. They have discovered a God who loves them more than they imagined and who strengthens them to face the challenges of today and the trials of tomorrow with incredible courage. He is the God of hope.

In a time of desperation the psalmist David cried out, "For You are my hope, O Lord God" (Psalm 71:5). Hope began for David where it begins for all of us. It began with the belief that there was a God in heaven who was bigger that his problems, greater than his difficulties, and larger than any challenge he might face. Without a knowledge of a God who cares for us, understands our pain, and heals our hurts, and who will one day defeat all the powers of hell and usher in a new world, we are left without hope to face life's challenges alone. It is this sense of God's presence, unconditional love, and constant care that fills our hearts with hope.

The Bible: The Book of Hope

The Bible is a book filled with hope. Its stories are about people like you and me. Sometimes they were strong and conquered mightily for God. At other times they were weak and failed miserably, but in each of these instances God was there to give them hope to face tomorrow. The word "hope" is used more than 125 times in the Bible. The apostle Paul, who faced so many challenging situations, used it more than 40 times. He was beaten, stoned, shipwrecked, and imprisoned, yet he was filled with hope. Writing to his friends living in Rome, he declared, "Now may the God of hope fill you with all joy and peace in believing, that you may abound in hope by the power of the Holy Spirit" (Romans 15:13). As we place our hope in a God who is bigger than any problem we ever face, our hearts are filled with "joy and peace in believing." The confidence that there is a God who loves us beyond what we can ever understand fills us with hope. There is never a circumstance that we face in life that God is not prepared to handle.

Hope That Does Not Disappoint

In Christ there is hope. There is never a challenge we find ourselves facing when there is not hope in Christ. There is an old hymn that says, "Just when I need Him, Jesus is near . . . just when I need Him most." This Christ, who has created us and cares for us, has redeemed us. We are twice His. When the beings He perfectly created rebelled against His will in Eden's garden, Love provided a way. There was hope for Adam's race. Jesus is the "Lamb slain from the foundation of the world" (Revelation 13:8). Heaven's plan of salvation echoed throughout the entire universe. God's own Son, Jesus Christ, left heaven and came to this rebel planet to reveal God's love to unnumbered worlds and satisfy the demands of justice. Where Adam failed, Jesus succeeded. In His life and death, He revealed the Father's love. He met the demands of the law and resisted Satan's most vicious temptations. He lived the perfect life we should have lived, and died the death we should have died. "The wages of sin is death, but the gift of God is eternal life in Christ Jesus our Lord" (Romans 6:23). His grace, forgiveness, and mercy flow from His heart of infinite love. Billy Graham put it well when he said, "God's mercy and grace give me hope—for myself, and for our world." As the song says: "My hope is built on nothing less than Jesus' blood and righteousness."

There is hope in Christ—hope that our sins are not too great to be forgiven, hope that our temptations are not too great to be overcome, hope that our challenges are not too great to be conquered, and hope that our tomorrows will be much better than today. Still Christ offers us more—much more—than the assurance that He is with us today. The hope that Christ offers is a hope that looks beyond this world to the next. It is the hope of His soon return. The apostle Paul beautifully blends Christ's first coming to earth to redeem us with His second coming to take us home. In an encouraging letter to his young friend Titus, the apostle declares that we are "looking for the blessed hope and glorious appearing of our great God and Savior Jesus Christ, who gave Himself for us, that He might redeem us from every lawless deed and purify for Himself His own special people, zealous for good works" (Titus 2:13, 14). Jesus came once to reveal the

Father's love and to earn the legal right to redeem us. He is coming a second time to claim His purchased possession.

Hope Beyond Tomorrow

Murdo Ewen MacDonald, a prisoner of war in Germany and chaplain to American soldiers, explained how he learned of the Normandy invasion. Early on D-Day he was awakened and told that a Scotsman in the British prisoner-of-war camp wanted to see him. MacDonald ran to the barbed wire that separated the two camps. The Scot, who was in touch with the BBC by underground radio, spoke two words in Gaelic, meaning "They have come!" MacDonald ran back to the American camp and spread the news: "They have come! They have come!" And everyone knew the Allied troops had landed at Normandy. The reaction was incredible. Men jumped and shouted, hugged each other, even rolled on the ground. Outwardly they were still captives, but inwardly they were free. That's the hope that changes our lives. One day we too will be delivered from this prison camp of sin and suffering. We will cry out, "He has come! He has come!" The Bible is filled with the best hope of all—the hope of our Lord's return. In more than 1,500 places the Bible speaks about the return of Christ. It is emphasized once in every 25 verses in the New Testament and for every prophecy about the first coming of Christ in the Old Testament, there are eight highlighting the second coming of Christ or the return of Christ to this world in glory. Here are just a few examples of the hopeful promises throughout the Bible of Christ's soon return.

Bible Predictions of Christ's Return

The first prediction of the return of Christ to this world is given by Enoch. There is no book of Enoch in the Bible, but in the New Testament the small book of Jude, just before Revelation, quotes Enoch. Enoch lived just before the great worldwide Flood. God took this righteous man to heaven bodily when he was 365 years old. Don't let Enoch's age surprise you, because before the Flood many biblical characters lived for more than 700 years, and some, including Adam and Methuselah, lived for more than 900 years. Adam was created by

God with enormous vital force and was designed to live forever, so Enoch's 365 years was far less than average for that time. Enoch is a type of those who will ascend to heaven in the sky when Jesus comes. Here is what the Bible says about Enoch's prediction of the coming of Christ.

"Enoch, the seventh from Adam, prophesied about these men also, saying, 'Behold, the Lord comes with ten thousands of His saints' " (Jude 14). More than 3,000 years before the first coming of Jesus, Enoch predicted that the Messiah would come not only as the suffering servant to die for our sins, but also as the conquering king who would come to deliver us from this sinful world and vanquish all evil.

The psalmist David adds his testimony by declaring, "Our God shall come, and shall not keep silent; a fire shall devour before Him, and it shall be very tempestuous all around Him" (Psalm 50:3).

The prophet Isaiah encourages us all to have hope. There is coming a day when Christ will return, and the forces of hell that cause so much disaster in our world will be defeated forever. In Isaiah 35 the prophet states, "Say to those who are fearful-hearted, 'Be strong, do not fear! Behold, your God will come with vengeance, with the recompense of God; He will come and save you' " (verse 4). The biblical prophets lived in hope, not despair. They looked beyond the challenges, trials, and difficulties they faced in their lives to a brand-new tomorrow. With prophetic insight and divine eyesight their view penetrated the future. They had absolute confidence that Christ would return, and that sin, suffering, heartache, sorrow, disease, and death would be no more.

Jesus' Own Promise

Just before Jesus ascended to heaven, He assured His followers, "I will come again." The fact that Jesus is coming to the world a second time is as certain as the reality that He lived on this earth 2,000 years ago. There is hope on the way. The promise of Christ's return rings with reassurance. The Savior encouraged His disciples with this promise: "Let not your heart be troubled; you believe in God, believe also in Me. In My Father's house are many mansions; if it were not so, I would have told you. I go to prepare a place for you. And if I go and prepare a place for you, I will come again and receive you to Myself; that where I am, there you may be also" (John 14:1-3).

66

Christ's comforting words are like a promissory note: Jesus said He would return—and we can bank on it! The second coming of Christ is not based on idle speculation. It is not based on a vain wish or human philosophy. It is based on the unchangeable, reliable, certain promises of God's Word. The second coming of Christ reveals the tremendous truth that all of history is moving toward one glorious climax. We have a final destiny. Life is going somewhere, and we are to meet Someone who has the ultimate answer to all of life's problems—and without this conviction, there is little left to live for.

Jesus' words come echoing down the centuries: "Let not your heart be troubled." Stop worrying. There is no need to be anxious. This world is not all there is. Cling to My promise. Trust My word. "You believe in God, believe also in Me. . . . I go to prepare a place for you. And . . . I will come again." The promise of Christ's soon return lifts our spirits. It encourages our hearts. It brightens our days. It illumines our nights. It makes every mountain we climb easier.

Notice a few expressions in this passage. They are going to encourage your heart. Jesus says, "In my Father's house are many mansions." The word "mansions" is better translated "abodes," "dwelling places," or "residences." Here is what Jesus is saying: "There is plenty of room in My eternal kingdom. There is no shortage of space. There is room for you."

The apostle John echoes these words in the Bible's last book, in Revelation 7:9: "After these things I looked, and behold, a great multitude which no one could number, of all nations, tribes, peoples, and tongues." Heaven has enough room for all. The sacrifice of Christ is enough for all. The cross of Calvary provides redemption for all who will receive it. Jesus is assuring His disciples that there is plenty of room in heaven for each one of them and that He will come back to take them to Himself. What does it mean that Jesus is preparing a place for us? It certainly does not mean that He is a construction foreman directing the angels how to build our heavenly mansions. Jesus ascends to heaven and, in the presence of the Father, receives the assurance that His sacrifice is accepted. The gates of heaven are opened for all humankind.

In light of the great controversy between good and evil in the universe, Jesus assures us that, through His grace and because of His death on the cross, we can live eternally with Him. He assures us that He will be our advocate, our defense attorney, in heaven's final judgment. Daniel 7 describes this cosmic judgment. There are 10,000 times 10,000 heavenly beings that gather around God's throne. Heaven's eternal records are open to the universe. With all-absorbing interest the entire universe watches. The destinies of the entire human race are now to be settled. Men and women will be eternally saved or eternally lost. Jesus steps forth in the judgment and declares that all those who by genuine faith have accepted His sacrifice and are transformed by His grace have both their title and fitness for heaven. The prophet Daniel triumphantly declares that "judgment was made in favor of the saints of the Most High" (Daniel 7:22). We are filled with hope because the One who died for us lives for us. Our joy overflows because the One who died for us and lives for us is coming again for us.

The Disciples Died Triumphantly in Hope

Think of the deaths of the disciples. It is commonly believed that each of them suffered a martyr's death, except John, but this is what we know for sure.

James was beheaded by Herod. Although he was the first of the apostles to suffer martyrdom, such a fate nevertheless did not quench his spirit or destroy his hope.

Peter was crucified upside down, likely in A.D. 66 by Nero's Roman guard. He died in hope. Here are his words: "Nevertheless we, according to His promise, look for new heavens and a new earth in which righteousness dwells" (2 Peter 3:13).

The apostle Paul spent years in a damp Roman dungeon and then was likely beheaded about the same time as Peter was martyred by Nero in A.D. 66. Yet filled with hope and assurance, he looked beyond what was to what will be. He believed that Christ had conquered the tomb and that one day Jesus would return as He had promised, to deliver him from the stranglehold of death. This courageous disciple of Christ clung to the promises of God's Word. He believed that "the Lord Himself will descend from heaven with a shout, with the voice of an archangel, and with the trumpet of God. And the dead in Christ shall rise first. Then we who are alive and remain shall be caught up together with them in the clouds to meet the Lord in the air. And thus we shall always be with the Lord" (1 Thessalonians 4:16, 17). The apostle Paul did not die a defeated, broken man. He was buoyed up by the promise of Christ's return, and died in hope.

Consider the apostle John. He was burned in a cauldron of boiling oil and as an old man in his 90s exiled to the island of Patmos by the emperor Domitian. During his exile on this lonely isle, Jesus Christ gave John a vision of His return. He wrote about that vision in the Bible's last book, Revelation. John's words are filled with hope: "Behold, He is coming with clouds, and every eye will see Him, even they who pierced Him. And all the tribes of the earth will mourn because of Him. Even so, Amen" (Revelation 1:7). Jesus' return to this world will certainly not be a secret event. Every eye will see Jesus when He returns. The eyes of the young, and the eyes of the old. The eyes of the educated, and the eyes of the uneducated; the eyes of the rich, and the eyes of the poor. People from all cultures, nationalities, languages, groups, and countries will see Him come.

Both the first chapter of Revelation and the last chapter ring with the certainty of Christ's return. On the last page of the Bible—in the last chapter of the last book—Jesus promises further: "And behold, I am coming quickly, and My reward is with Me, to give to every one according to his work" (Revelation 22:12).

Each one of the disciples, except John, died a martyr's death, yet they were triumphant. They were faithful in the face of incredibly challenging circumstances. They were filled with an inner peace that "surpasses all understanding" (Philippians 4:7). They clung to Christ's Word. They believed Christ's promise: "I will come again!" The words of the angels at Christ's ascension rang in their ears. "Now when He had spoken these things, while they watched, He was taken up, and a cloud received Him out of their sight. And while they looked steadfastly toward heaven as He went up, behold, two men [angels] stood by them in white apparel, who also said, 'Men of Galilee, why do you stand gazing up into heaven? This same Jesus, who was taken up from you into heaven, will so come in like manner as you saw Him go into heaven' " (Acts 1:9-11).

Don't miss the fact that on this occasion angels, as heavenly messengers from God, confirmed Christ's promise and testified to its literal truthfulness: "This same Jesus" was not a ghostly spirit, but had "flesh and bones," to use Jesus' own words (Luke 24:39). He "will so come in like manner" as He ascended to heaven. Jesus' ascension to heaven was a real, literal event. His return will again be a very real, literal event. Soon He is coming again to take us home.

Every challenge you face, every difficulty you experience, every trial you meet, will soon be over. Cling to the promise of Jesus' soon return, let your heart soar with hope, and let peace flood your soul. The Bible is a book of hope, because there is a day after the day after tomorrow. There is something beyond this life. We have this hope that burns within our hearts—the hope of the coming of our Lord. And that hope is enough to see us through all of life's challenges.

"Then the sign of the Son of Man will appear in heaven, and then all the tribes of the earth will mourn, and they will see the Son of Man coming on the clouds of heaven with power and great glory. And He will send His angels with a great sound of a trumpet, and they will gather together His elect from the four winds, from one end of heaven to the other" (Matthew 24:30, 31).

The Bible constantly points us to a better tomorrow. It holds out the promise that one day Jesus Christ will return. Evil will be destroyed. Righteousness will reign forever. Sin, sickness, and suffering will be no more. Disease, disaster, and death will be vanquished. Wickedness, war, and worry will vanish away. The apostle Paul calls this glorious event "the blessed hope" (Titus 2:13). What a hope! Jesus Christ will return. Death will not have the last word; Jesus will. One day soon our loved ones who have died believing in and living for Christ will be resurrected from their graves to see Him face to face. One day soon the hopes of all the ages will be realized. Jesus Christ will return, and we who are alive to experience this spectacular, glorious event will be caught up to meet Him in the air. We will travel with Him on the most amazing space journey ever to the most amazing place in the universe and live with Him throughout all eternity.

We need not worry about the future. We do not have to let fear grip our hearts and strangle our joy. Christ has created us. Christ has redeemed us. Christ cares for us. Christ sustains us, and Christ is coming again to take us home. Now, that is something to be hopeful about.

CHAPTER 7

HOW TO SURVIVE WHEN THE ECONOMY COLLAPSES

We are just beginning to experience the long-term economic consequences of COVID-19 on our personal lives and our families. The short-term consequences with thousands dead and hundreds of thousands more sick were bad enough, but there are significant additional consequences that society now faces. The economic impact of the pandemic is hitting many families full force. Many of the unemployed during the crisis are going back to work, but they are still experiencing the effects of lost income from their time off, and the debts they incurred. The stock market plummeted during the pandemic, with millions of people losing almost all their life savings. The entire world economy is on extremely shaky footing, and we wonder whether life will ever be the same. The economic picture for the foreseeable future is dire. Many of the businesses forced to shut down because of the lockdowns may never recover. In a report to Adventist Church leaders, investment specialist Tim Aka made this astute observation: "Many people are living paycheck to paycheck with little or no savings." The results of the coronavirus pandemic has thrown them into a financial dilemma. Unemployment rates in the United States reached more than 20 percent, the highest level since 1934. Europe's Gross National Product dropped nearly 15 percent in the second quarter of 2020 alone. One report indicates that "[the United States'] and Eurozone's economies could take until 2023 to recover from the impact of the COVID-19 coronavirus crisis, according to a new report from consultancy McKinsey & Company."

Latin America and the Caribbean will see the largest contraction in economic activity in its history in 2020, because of the impact of the novel coronavirus (COVID-19) pandemic, a United Nations agency warned on Tuesday, April 21, 2020. According to the Economic

Commission for Latin America and the Caribbean (ECLAC), based in Santiago, Chile, the combined effect of pandemic-hit external and domestic factors "will lead to the worst contraction that the region has ever undergone." This simply means more people will be out of work, more companies will go bankrupt, more families will be under enormous financial stress, and more countries will struggle to provide basic services for their populations. The poor and underprivileged will suffer the most. Because they are dependent on their daily wages and have no savings accounts, they are often unable to provide even the necessities of life for their families.

The international markets have experienced a serious downturn. Dozens of countries could soon suffer from devastating famines as a result of the coronavirus, an official with the United Nations said.

Famines of "biblical proportions" may be experienced in the coming months because of such factors as reductions in foreign aid, the price of oil, and tourism, according to David Beasley, director of the UN's World Food Programmed Branch.

"There are no famines yet," Beasley said. "But I must warn you that if we don't prepare and act now—to secure access, avoid funding shortfalls and disruptions to trade—we could be facing multiple famines of biblical proportions within a few short months." "Millions of civilians living in conflict-scarred nations, including many women and children, face being pushed to the brink of starvation, with the specter of famine a very real and dangerous possibility" (New York *Daily News*, April 22, 2020).

Confronting the Issues

What impact will all of this have on our personal finances? How will this impact our families? What impact will this disruption in society have on our mental health? What long-term consequences might there be on our physical health? Most of all, what can we do to survive the catastrophic consequences of COVID-19 and other pandemics or catastrophes that strike us? This is not the first disaster that has ever hit our world, and it will not be the last. How can we stay strong amid these worldwide epidemics and natural disasters that are striking our world with increasing frequency? In this chapter we will focus on four specific areas of survival: (1) How you can survive financially in a time of crisis; (2) How your family and especially your children can survive; (3) How you can survive physically; (4) How you can survive emotionally.

How to Survive a Financial Crash

In the sixth century before Christ the wealthiest man in the world was Croesus. Croesus was the king of Lydia from 560 to 547 B.C. He is credited with issuing the first true gold coins with a standardized purity for general circulation.

One day King Croesus asked the philosopher Solon who the happiest man in the world was. Solon's answer as recorded by the Greek historian Herodotus went something like this: "To live well, you must prepare to die well." There is something tragically wrong with a society that is obsessed with making money. Seeking happiness in material things leads us down the road to nowhere. Attempting to fill our lives with things only leaves us empty. Solon was right. There is more to life than simply making money.

Norman Cousins, editor of *Saturday Review*, made a very perceptive statement 40 years ago. It was true then, but it is even truer now. "We are so busy extending ourselves and increasing the size and ornamentation of our personal kingdom that we have hardly considered that no age in history has had so many loose props under it as our own." We are so busy buying that we have failed to realize that there are some moral screws loose in our society. The foundation is cracking. We might just be investing our money in the wrong places.

The Bible presents eternal financial principles that make sense. It reveals financial secrets that most of the world does not know. It encourages us to reevaluate our priorities—to seek the eternal rather than the earthly. God's Word leads us to make investments that will pay off in the long run. Here are three financial principles outlined in the Bible that will enable you to survive any financial crisis.

1. Accept the eternal truth that God is the Creator of this world and the owner of everything in it.

In Psalm 50 David records God's words to him at a time of great need. God reminds him that He is the Creator and in charge of this world in these words:

"Every beast of the forest is Mine, and the cattle on a thousand hills. I know all the birds of the mountains, and the wild beasts of the field are Mine. If I were hungry, I would not tell you; for the world is Mine, and all its fullness" (Psalm 50:10-12).

David responds to the marvel of God's Creation in Psalm 104.

"O Lord, how manifold are Your works! In wisdom You have made them all. The earth is full of Your possessions—this great and wide sea, in which are innumerable teeming things, living things both small and great" (Psalm 104:24, 25).

Isaiah the prophet adds that the world is God's not only because He created it, but because He redeemed it. "Thus says the Lord, who created you, O Jacob, and He who formed you, O Israel: 'Fear not, for I have redeemed you; I have called you by your name; you are Mine' " (Isaiah 43:1).

When our Lord created this world, He entrusted it to Adam. God gave Adam dominion over the entire creation (see Genesis 1:26). When Adam sinned in Eden, he surrendered his right of dominion. Lucifer, the fallen angel, usurped the dominion and claimed the lordship of the earth. Bible writers often refer to Lucifer as the "prince of this world" or "the prince of the power of the air" (see John 12:31; 14:30; Ephesians 2:2). Christ's sinless life and substitutionary death fully paid the ransom for our sin. At the cross Satan's fate was sealed, and complete restoration pledged for this planet (see Ephesians 1:14; 1 Corinthians 6:19, 20; John 12:31, 32). God is the true owner of this world, both by creation and redemption. Everything we have is a gift of His grace. We are stewards of goods entrusted to us by God. We are and were Christ's. He created us, and He redeemed us. This world is His. He made it in the first place and shed His blood to redeem it. Understanding this concept—that Christ created us and redeemed us—makes all the difference. What we have is really not our own. Moses admonishes us to "remember the Lord your God, for it is He who gives you power to get wealth, that He may establish His covenant which He swore to your fathers, as it is this day" (Deuteronomy 8:18). The talents we have to make money come from God. The ability to work comes from God. Every breath we take comes from God. He is the one who opens doors of opportunity for us to survive economically. He is our provider, our sustainer, and our supporter. What we have is a gift of His grace. Everything we have is His because He has created us and redeemed us. We are stewards of His possessions, not owners. The apostle Paul clarifies this point in these words: "It is required in stewards that one be found faithful" (1 Corinthians 4:2).

A steward is one who manages another person's property, finances, or other affairs. And that is what we are—stewards—under God. For we do not own this world or anything in it; God, as Creator, owns it all. Yet He placed Adam and Eve and their descendants in charge of it all by giving them "dominion" over the other creatures and by placing them "in the Garden of Eden to tend and keep it" (Genesis 1:28; 2:15). But Paul teaches us that as stewards we are required to "found faithful" in everything we manage, including finances. Jesus adds, "He who is faithful in what is least is faithful also in much; and he who is unjust in what is least is unjust also in much" (Luke 16:10).

Godfrey Davis, who wrote a biography about the duke of Wellington, said, "I found an old account ledger that showed how the duke spent his money. It was a far better clue to what he thought was really important than the reading of his letters or speeches."

How we handle money reveals much about the depth of our commitment to Christ. That's why Jesus often talked about money. One-sixth of the gospels, including one out of every three parables, touches on stewardship. Jesus wasn't a fundraiser. He dealt with money matters because money matters. For some of us, though, it matters too much (*Our Daily Bread*, August 26, 1993).

2. Believe that the God who created you and redeemed you cares for you and will provide for you.

In Philippians 4:19 we have an eternal pledge: "And my God shall supply all your need according to His riches in glory by Christ Jesus." To all who are faithful stewards, God gives the assurance of supplying their needs. The needs of God's children are already underwritten by the bank of heaven. Jesus stated, "Therefore do not worry, saying, 'What shall we eat?' or . . . 'What shall we wear?' . . . But seek first the kingdom of God and His righteousness, and all these things shall be added to you" (Matthew 6:31-33).

A pandemic does not eradicate the promises of God. COVID-19 has not erased the assurance of God's eternal Word. The coronavirus need not cause a crisis of confidence in God's ability to solve our problems and provide for our needs. It can lead us to deeper faith, greater trust, and more secure confidence in God. Amid our greatest challenges, God's promises are still there.

I have seen this powerfully demonstrated in my own life. My father became a Seventh-day Adventist when I was 13 years old. As the result of his commitment to keep the Bible Sabbath, he lost his job. In addition to that, Dad made the decision to be faithful in returning his tithe and offerings. To meet the needs of our family, Dad worked three part-time jobs. Life was not easy, but I often remember him quoting two Bible promises.

When I wondered how God would provide for us, in his quiet, confident manner Dad would first quote Matthew 6:33: "But seek first the kingdom of God and His righteousness, and all these things shall be added to you." And then he would add Philippians 4:19: "And my God shall supply all your need according to His riches in glory by Christ Jesus." Dad's faithfulness and settled confidence in God gave our entire family the assurance that in our time of trial God would come through, and He did. We may not have had all the luxuries of some families, but we had something worth much more: a father who was faithful to God and who gave us the assurance that we could trust God with the totality of our lives. When times are tough and our finances are limited, trusting God in these trying times is an act of faith. It is saying, "God, I believe You can care for me. I place my life in Your hands. I believe Your promises." Giving is a tangible expression of our faith.

The very essence of the Christian life is trust. It is trusting God with our finances, our health, our time, and our very lives. It is faith that the living Christ who has provided us salvation through His grace and power through His Holy Spirit will fulfill His promise to supply our needs. It is trusting, even during a global pandemic that may touch our lives and the lives of those we love.

When we trust God in trying times, it gives God the opportunity to do for us "exceedingly abundantly above all that we ask or think" (Ephesians 3:20). It opens the door of our hearts to receive His abundant blessings. Faith enables the riches of heaven to flow into our lives from His abundant storehouse of grace. God is still in control in every crisis. A terribly devastating pandemic does not wipe out His promises. Living lives of trust, we are secure in His love today, tomorrow, and forever.

3. Choose to reorder your priorities in view of the coming of Jesus.

The Bible makes some remarkable predictions regarding an economic crash during the last days of earth's history. The greatest treasure we can have is a personal relationship with Jesus Christ—the Pearl of Great Price. He offers us abundant joy, inner peace, and lasting satisfaction. The fleeting pleasures of this world are soon to pass away. When our happiness, contentment, and security come from our material possessions, and then the economy suddenly crashes, we are left discouraged, downhearted, and depressed; but when our faith is anchored in Jesus and the eternal treasures of His Word, we are secure. The apostle James reveals the last-day delusion and disappointment of those who have made a god of their money.

"Now listen, you rich people, weep and wail because of the misery that is coming on you. Your wealth has rotted, and moths have eaten your clothes. Your gold and silver are corroded. Their corrosion will testify against you and eat your flesh like fire. You have hoarded wealth in the last days. Look! The wages you failed to pay the workers who mowed your fields are crying out against you. The cries of the harvesters have reached the ears of the Lord Almighty. You have lived on earth in luxury and self-indulgence. You have fattened yourselves in the day of slaughter" (James 5:1-5, NIV).

In an article published on November 19, 2020, for the online magazine *The Balance Everyday*, titled "Lottery Curse Victims: Seven People Who Won Big and Lost Everything," author Sandra Grauschopf describes the devastating results to seven entire families who won the lottery. Family relations deteriorated. Lavish spending replaced frugal living. Greed consumed their joy, and very often drug or alcohol abuse followed.

When a family in New York won the Irish Sweepstakes, they were overjoyed. Dad was a steamfitter. Johnny, who was 26 years old, loaded crates on docks. Tim was going to night school. Dad split the million with his sons. They all said the money wouldn't change their plans. During the following year, conflict erupted in the family. The boys weren't speaking to their father or to one another. Johnny spent his portion of the winnings on expensive racehorses; Tim spent it on lavish parties and the women he dated. Mom accused Dad of hiding his portion of the lottery winning from her. Within two years all of them were in court for nonpayment of income taxes. "It's the devil's own money," Mom said. Both the boys were drinking excessively and were on track to become alcoholics (from Chuck Rasmussen, "Winning the Lottery").

When our happiness is dependent on the amount of money we have, we are chasing a mirage. Money provides only temporary satisfaction and superficial happiness.

The book of Revelation describes an economic collapse that is coming just before the return of Jesus. Those who have trusted their money as a source of happiness will be greatly disappointed. What they have lived for will quickly vanish. Their dreams will be dashed. Revelation 18 predicts a sudden economic collapse that stuns the world. Revelation 18:17-19 says that the merchants of the earth are weeping, because in "one hour such great riches came to nothing." The antichrist power has attempted to unite humanity around a counterfeit day of worship. In an attempt to usher in world peace and security, it has established a confederacy of religious, political, and economic powers. Natural disasters, economic collapse, political conflicts, and social chaos only harden hearts and make the antichrist more determined to accomplish its purposes.

While God sends an appeal to the entire world to unite with His true commandment-keeping people, this union of church, state, and economic powers says, " 'I sit as queen, and am no widow, and will not see sorrow.' Therefore her plagues will come in one day—death and mourning and famine. And she will be utterly burned with fire, for strong is the Lord God who judges her" (verses 7, 8). Verse 19 adds, "In one hour she is made desolate."

The great confederacy of evil persists in its opposition to God and is blind to what is about to happen. The kings and the merchants—the political and economic interests that have united themselves with this apostate religious system—mourn her fall. They united with her and lived luxuriously because of her as they exercised power over the earth. Now they fall with her and mourn as they suffer God's punishment. They do not mourn for their sins and their rebellion against God. They mourn because of the consequences of their sins. Suddenly there is an unprecedented economic collapse, and in one hour their riches come to nothing. They have placed their confidence in the wrong place. They have trusted in their wealth and material possessions rather than placing their trust in the promises of God. This leads us to a very practical question. How can our families survive an economic crisis?

Your Family Can Survive Tough Times

There was a massive study done in the United States involving families across America on the impact of the coronavirus crisis titled, "Snapshot of the COVID Crisis Impact on Working Families." The study was authored by public policy and economics scholars at Barnard College, Columbia University (in New York City), and the Sanford School of Public Policy at Duke University (in Durham, North Carolina), Elizabeth O. Ananat and Anna Gassman-Pines. The study was published on the Econofact Network on March 30, 2020. It proposed that "the outbreak of the novel coronavirus will deeply impact many American families." We might add that although this study was done on the impact of family life in the United States, its results will be replicated in countries around the world.

As of March 25, 2020, 21 percent of the people studied reported being permanently laid off, while another 20 percent gave an account of being temporarily laid off. A majority of the sample, 55 percent, indicated that someone in their household had been laid off. Of those who were able to keep their jobs at that time, 51 percent experienced reduced hours. These numbers, according to the study, were more severe and happened more quickly than what took place during the Great Depression, which started in 1929.

Willie and Elaine Oliver, family life specialists, write, "To be sure, when a family experiences the loss of income, this reality is associated with high levels of anxiety and depression, in addition to other mental health challenges. Sadly, these mental health effects of job loss are not likely to be short-term. Prior studies have discovered significant surges in both adult and youth suicide resulting from economic recessions. In fact, mental health tends to decline significantly, even among those who do not experience family loss of employment, even when the rates of unemployment are much smaller than we are experiencing during this pandemic. It is worthy of note that these outcomes impact other areas of life, including triggering lower levels of student test scores and causing lower levels of college attendance among those who live through these experiences during adolescence. These cumulative consequences, in the short term and long term, are more remarkable for disadvantaged populations, resulting in health disparities and achievement gaps, which are already larger and are more likely to increase."

Satan, the archenemy of Jesus, is the originator of every evil in the world. Whether working through the Pharisees and other religious leaders of His day to undermine the work of God on behalf of the salvation of sinners, or being the cause of a pandemic that is robbing millions of their lives, livelihood, and future well-being, the devil is always up to no good. The good news, to be sure, is that God is not like an absentee landlord that has left us to fend for ourselves. Rather, He sent Jesus that we might have the abundant life, regardless of the assaults of the evil one.

Despite the incredible pressure economic crises put on families, there are things parents can do to keep themselves and their children sane during this time of instability and unpredictability. Willie and Elaine Oliver make these practical suggestions:

1. Ask your children what they are thinking about, and simply listen. Even if they say things that may alarm you because they might be true, don't be alarmed or allow it to show on your face.

Your children need a safe place to talk and an opportunity to express their feelings, and it is up to you to provide this space.

2. Set the example you want to be followed in your home. Take care of yourself spiritually, physically, and emotionally by spending time with God, exercising, eating nutritious food, and thinking positive thoughts. Practice being patient and kind, as is written in Scripture (see 1 Corinthians 13:4).

3. Pray with your children on a regular basis. Allow your thoughts to be turned to God, who has promised never to leave you (see Matthew 28:20); to keep you in perfect peace (see Isaiah 26:3); and to provide all your needs (see Philippians 4:19).

How to Survive Physically During Tough Times

When our finances are in serious trouble, it takes a toll on both our own physical health and the physical health of our families. Pandemics bring with them serious consequences, even after the pandemic is over. Researchers have clearly shown a correlation between poor health and declining life spans for months if not years after a major influenza or some other catastrophic health crisis. They have also discovered basic health principles to enable us to survive in times of crisis. Most deaths during the COVID-19 pandemic were from those having such pre-existing conditions as heart disease, hypertension, high blood pressure, diabetes, or obesity. Simply put, the stronger your immune system, the greater your possibility of surviving a pandemic. The better your physical health when the crisis breaks, the better your possibility of surviving.

On April 20, 2020, the European Journal of Clinical Nutrition published an article on the role of nutrition and our health habits in surviving a pandemic.

The authors stated, "At the individual level, the common denominator that drives most of the nutrition and dietary recommendations to combat viral infections, including COVID-19, lies within the link between diet and immunity. In fact, existing evidence highlights that diet has a profound effect on people's immune system and disease susceptibility."

"Therefore, the responsibility of the individuals during the COVID-19 pandemic lies in making an effort to choose a healthy lifestyle, eat diets high in fruits and vegetables, exercise during free time, try to maintain a healthy weight, and get an adequate amount of sleep. In addition to taking care of one's dietary intake, the collective responsibility of individuals is to avoid the spread of misinformation related to nutrition and dietary intake, and the COVID-19."

The article goes on to make these eight recommendations. Consider these recommendations as survival guidelines for any health crisis.

1. Try to eat well-balanced meals.
2. Avoid irregular snacking.
3. Choose food rich in vitamins A, C, E, B_6, B_{12}, zinc, and iron, such as citrus fruits, dark-green leafy vegetables, nuts, and dairy products.
4. Maintain a healthy lifestyle of exercise at home.
5. Get adequate sleep.
6. Spend time meditating.
7. Avoid smoking, alcohol, and drugs.
8. Don't buy into quack or unscientific miracle cures.

God's intention for you is to both survive and thrive during times of crisis. This is why He says, "I pray that you may prosper in all things and be in health, just as your soul prospers" (3 John 2). Although we live in a broken world of sin, suffering, and sickness, and we cannot always avoid disease, God's intent is for us to, as far as possible, live healthy lives. As we make positive choices, our immune systems will strengthen and our health will improve. It is never too late to begin making the best possible health choices for ourselves and our families.

How to Survive Emotionally During Tough Times

Worry and anxiety have gripped millions of people. They are afraid that the coronavirus or some other disease may strike them next. They heard about the rising death toll and trembled with fear. They were concerned about their children or grandchildren or elderly parents, and many of them still are. Or possibly it's financial fear. Many people are worried that they may not be able to pay their rent or their mortgage. They are concerned about a business that has closed, and are fearful they will not have a job when this pandemic is over. For some it is even more dire—they are concerned about how to feed their families. They are on edge filled with uncertainty about the future. The answer to crippling fear is trust in God's love, care, and provisions for us.

The Word of God provides real-life examples of God's people in crisis and how they developed deeper trust in trying times. These biblical stories reveal eternal principles that are faith building. They were written in another time and another place, but they speak to us at this time and in this place. They were written centuries ago, but speak with relevance in the twenty-first century to a world devastated by a devastating, death-dealing pandemic.

God Is Still in Control in Times of Crisis

Judah faced a crisis. Devastation and death were at its door. Catastrophe seemed certain. The great Assyrian king Tiglath-pileser III was on a rampage to conquer the Middle East. He had already conquered much of western Asia. Uzziah, king of Judah, was the leading figure of resistance against Assyrian aggression. Uzziah had reigned for 52 years (791-739 B.C.). During Uzziah's reign the nation prospered. Desert areas were reclaimed. Jerusalem's walls were fortified. The nation expanded its territory. Judah's prosperity was largely because of Uzziah's faithfulness to God, but in an act of arrogance and presumption he attempted to burn incense in the temple and was immediately stricken with leprosy and eventually died. The nation was devastated. Their long-time ruler was dead. Doom seemed certain. All hope of resisting the apparently invincible Assyrian armies danced away like a shadow. The nation's inhabitants were paralyzed by fear. An enemy invader was approaching, and there seemed little they could do about it. They were helpless and hopeless.

At the time of this catastrophe, Isaiah writes, "In the year that King Uzziah died, I saw the Lord sitting on a throne, high and lifted up, and the train of His robe filled the temple" (Isaiah 6:1). In the midst of a crisis heaven's throne is not vacant. God reassured His people that He was still in control. He was still sovereign. The crisis did not catch God by surprise. God has not left us alone in times of our greatest trials. Pandemics rage, but God is still on His throne. An enemy invader, COVID-19, ravaged the land, but in these trying times we can learn lessons of trust. When fear gives way to trust, peace floods into our lives. Isaiah the prophet reassured God's people with a powerful promise. His message comes echoing and reechoing down the corridors of time: "You will keep him in perfect peace, whose mind is stayed on You, because he trusts in You. Trust in the Lord forever" (Isaiah 26:3, 4). The simple key to surviving any crisis we face is trust—believing that the Creator of the universe, the Redeemer of this world, and our living Lord, loves us and cares for us no matter what we are facing or ever will face.

When disease ravages our land, when our bodies are racked with fever, when life seems to be falling apart, we can still trust. We can trust that through His Holy Spirit, God is with us. He is strengthening us, encouraging us, supporting us, giving us hope of a better tomorrow, pointing us to the day when sickness, suffering, and heartache will be no more.

CHAPTER 8

A PLACE OF ETERNAL SECURITY

Imagine two young men in their 20s chopping firewood in the days of ancient Israel 3,000 years ago. Let's call them Ehud and Eli. As they gather wood for the evening's fire, they share stories, laugh together, and discuss their futures. Then it happens. As Ehud carelessly swings the ax with all his force, he misses his target slightly. The ax handle shatters, and the axhead flies with lightning speed and hits Eli in the throat. He is bleeding profusely, and there is little Ehud can do to save his friend's life. Although it was an accident, Ehud recognizes that his life will be taken next. Eli's father and brothers must avenge Eli's death by taking the life of his killer—that is, unless Ehud can make it to one of Israel's six cities of refuge.

There is no time to waste. Ehud begins to run, and as he picks up speed, he runs faster and still faster. His lungs are burning. He pants, almost out of breath. His legs ache. His heart is racing. Beads of sweat pour down his forehead. He forces himself to run even faster. In the distance he hears the galloping hooves of horses. Eli's father and brothers are in hot pursuit. He knows that if he does not make it to the city of refuge soon, his life is over. Consumed with guilt for his carelessness, overcome with worry, and filled with anxiety, he rushes on.

There were six of these cities of refuge scattered throughout Israel. The farthest anyone could ever be from the cities of refuge was one day's journey. The cities of refuge were established to give individuals who had accidentally killed someone a place of safety. The roads leading to these cities were kept in good repair, and there were signs posted all along the way pointing to the city with one word etched upon them: "Refuge."

We read about these cities in the Old Testament book of Joshua: "These were the cities appointed for all the children of Israel and for the stranger who dwelt among them, that whoever killed a person accidentally might flee there, and not die by the hand of the avenger of blood until he stood before the congregation" (Joshua 20:9). Any individual who killed another accidentally could flee to the city of refuge, present a case, and have a safe haven.

Commenting on these cities of refuge, the book *Patriarchs and Prophets* states, "He who fled to the city of refuge could make no delay. Family and employment were left behind. There was no time to say farewell to loved ones. His life was at stake, and every other interest must be sacrificed to the one purpose—to reach the place of safety. Weariness was forgotten, difficulties were unheeded. The fugitive dared not for one moment slacken his pace until he was within the wall of the city" (p. 517).

As Ehud raced to the city, the gates opened wide, and he was welcomed warmly. Inside the city Ehud found refuge, security, peace, and sanctuary. What an illustration of the refuge and sanctuary Christ offers us. Chased by guilt, attacked by fear, pursued by anxiety, and sought after by worry, we too can flee to a place of refuge—our sanctuary.

The cities of refuge were accessible to all, so God has created a sanctuary of refuge accessible to all. Our High Priest, Jesus, dwells in the heavenly sanctuary, a place of refuge and security, inviting us by faith to enter in and find refuge, hope, peace, freedom from anxiety, and calm.

Jesus' Invitation

Catastrophic events may shake this earth. Wars, international conflict, and national strife may ravage whole nations. Earthquakes may devastate entire cities, fierce tornadoes may destroy neighborhoods, floods may cause havoc with entire communities, pestilences may destroy the crops, and the coronavirus may spread with lightning speed around the world, killing tens of thousands. At times our hearts may quake with fear. We long for security. We want a safe place. We want to be sheltered from life's storms. When it appears that there is no place to hide, Jesus invites us by faith to look away from earth's trauma and find strength in heaven's sanctuary—His city of refuge.

Writing in the book of Hebrews, the apostle Paul encourages us with these words: "Seeing then that we have a great High Priest who has passed through the heavens, Jesus the Son of God, let us hold fast our confession. For we do not have a High Priest who cannot sympathize with our weaknesses, but was in all points tempted as we are, yet without sin. Let us therefore come boldly to the throne of grace, that we may obtain mercy and find grace to help in time of need" (Hebrews 4:14-16). Jesus, the one who died for us, lives for us. He experienced all the trials, temptations, and trauma that we experience, but to an infinitely greater degree. There is nothing in our human experience that He does not understand and has not gone through. He invites us to come into His presence by faith in heaven's sanctuary and find "grace to help in time of need." Do you have a time of need? Do you long for a safe place—a place of refuge and security? Jesus invites you to come.

Immediate Access to the Father

The central message of Jesus' high-priestly ministry in heaven's sanctuary is that through Him we have access to the Father. We have access to the Father because of Jesus Christ, who intercedes for us. There is no experience in life that we go through that our heavenly High Priest has not already experienced in kind and does not understand. Our High Priests understands us. Our High Priest identifies with us. Our High Priest has overcome for us. Our High Priest pardons us, releases us, and empowers us. Hebrews 7:25 adds, "Therefore He is also able to save to the uttermost those who come to God through Him, since He always lives to make intercession for them."

The Scriptures reveal that each one of us has a city of refuge. "Thus God, determining to show more abundantly to the heirs of promise the immutability of His counsel, confirmed it by an oath, that by two immutable things, in which it is impossible for God to lie, we might have strong consolation, who have fled for refuge to lay hold of [seize or grasp] the hope set before us. This hope we have as an anchor of the soul, both sure and steadfast, and which enters the Presence behind the veil, where the forerunner has entered for us, even Jesus, having become High Priest forever according to the order of Melchizedek"

(Hebrews 6:17-20). By faith we enter with Jesus, our heavenly high priest, into the sanctuary on high. Echoing and reechoing down the corridors of time, these words speak hope to our hearts. By faith we can soar into eternity. By faith we can dwell in heavenly places in Christ. By faith we can find in the heavenly sanctuary a place of refuge and security.

Be gone, guilt! Step aside, fear! Move over, anxiety! Vanish, worry! I am encircled in His love, enraptured in His presence, and anchored by faith in His sanctuary. In Christ there is security. In Christ there is refuge. In Christ we dwell in heavenly places (see Ephesians 1:3). Through Christ we have access to all our heavenly Father's love, grace, and power. Through Christ we enter the Father's presence by faith in heaven's sanctuary and find refuge. In all of life's challenges these promises are ours:

"The eternal God is your refuge" (Deuteronomy 33:27).

"God is our refuge and strength, a very present help in trouble" (Psalm 46:1).

"I have become as a wonder to many, but You are my strong refuge" (Psalm 71:7).

American Civil War Story of Access to the President

During the War Between the States, a young soldier in the Union Army lost his older brother and his father in the battle of Gettysburg. The soldier decided to go to Washington, D.C., to see President Lincoln to ask for an exemption from military service so that he could go back and help his sister and mother with the spring planting on the farm. When he arrived in Washington, after having received a furlough from the military to go and plead his case, he went to the White House, approached the front gate, and asked to see the president.

The guard on duty told him, "You can't see the president, young man! Don't you know there's a war going on? The president is a very busy man! Now go away, son! Get back out there on the battle lines, where you belong!"

So the young soldier left, very disheartened, and was sitting on a park bench not far from the White House when a little boy came up to him. The lad said, "Soldier, you look unhappy. What's wrong?" The soldier looked at the little boy and began to spill his heart to him. He told of his father and his brother being killed in the war, and of the desperate situation at home. He explained that his mother and sister had no one to help them with the farm. The little boy listened and said, "I can help you, soldier." He took the soldier by the hand and led him back to the front gate of the White House. Apparently, the guard didn't notice them, because they weren't stopped. They walked straight to the front door of the White House and walked right in. After they got inside, they walked right past generals and high-ranking officials, and no one said a word. The soldier couldn't understand this. Why didn't anyone try to stop them?

Finally, they reached the Oval Office—where the president was working—and the little boy didn't even knock on the door. He just walked right in and led the soldier in with him. There behind the desk was Abraham Lincoln and his secretary of state, looking over battle plans that were laid out on his desk.

The president looked at the boy and then at the soldier and said, "Good afternoon, Tad. Can you introduce me to your friend?"

And Tad Lincoln, the son of the president, said, "Daddy, this soldier needs to talk to you." The soldier pleaded his case before Mr. Lincoln, and right then and there he received the exemption that he desired. Tad Lincoln, the president's son, did not have to beg or plead to see his father. He didn't have to knock on the door. He walked right in, and his father was happy to see him. Jesus has immediate access to His Father and takes us by the hand and leads us directly into His presence.

Looking to Jesus, we are secure. Where we look makes all the difference in our Christian lives. If we dwell on our past, we often will be filled with a sense of failure. If we look within our own hearts, we often will be filled with a sense of inadequacy. If we are overly concerned about the future, we may be filled with a sense of worry. Looking to Jesus in heaven's eternal sanctuary, we discover our true sense of peace. By faith we rest in His love in heaven's city of refuge. In His arms we are secure now and forever.

The Sabbath: A Quiet Refuge

In addition to the heavenly sanctuary that we enter by faith in Jesus to find a place of refuge and security in this broken world, our loving heavenly Father has created a place of security and refuge here on this earth. The Jewish author Abraham Heschel calls it God's "palace in time." Each week God invites us to experience rest and find refuge in the midst of this out-of-control, hectic world. We can leave the cares of life aside as we enter God's Sabbath rest.

At Creation, centuries before the existence of the Jewish race, God set aside the seventh-day Sabbath. The first book of the Bible, Genesis, states, "And on the seventh day God ended His work which He had done, and He rested on the seventh day from all His work which He had done. Then God blessed the seventh day and sanctified it, because in it He rested from all His work which God had created and made" (Genesis 2:2, 3). In the book of Exodus the Word of God tells us that God "rested and was refreshed" on the seventh day at the end of Creation week (Exodus 31:17). When we enter God's rest on the seventh-day Sabbath, as commanded in Exodus 20:8-11, we too are refreshed. The Sabbath is an oasis in time, a place of quietness, peace, and security in an out-of-control wild world.

The Sabbath beautifully represents a forever relationship with God. It stretches from the Garden of Eden at Creation to the garden that God will make of this planet at the end of time. It stretches from Paradise lost to Paradise restored. We need that kind of forever in our lives. We need a place that reassures us that we are in an eternal relationship with the heavenly Father. We need a "palace in time" where that assurance can sink in deep, a place that says our heavenly Father will always be there for us. In the Sabbath we can find a sense of contented rest. Mental health specialist Torben Bergland has reviewed studies from a variety of sources on the impact of crisis and especially economic recessions on mental health. The research indicates that these societal catastrophes lead to higher rates of depression, anxiety, and suicide. Dr. Bergland then makes this insightful observation: "It's time for a time-out. We live in a world that is so rushed and high-paced that every second may be filled with something. Many are busy producing or consuming, one or the other, almost every waking moment. This leaves little time to think, to reflect, to meditate, to feel, to talk, to connect. As many things now stop, we need to slow down. To allow spaces to open up, to pause, to question, to evaluate, to reconsider. Don't stuff open spaces with whatever is at hand. Allow reflection to enter. Am I living the life I want to live? What are the real values and priorities of my life?" This is precisely the reason we need the Sabbath experience at this moment in time. It is a time to reflect, to meditate on the purpose of life, to get in touch with our Creator. On Sabbath we connect with our roots as children of God. We can grow and mature there. Yes, we need that kind of forever place that ties the whole of our lives to an eternal relationship with God. The Sabbath calls us from the things of time to the things of eternity. The Sabbath reminds us that we are not merely skin covering bones. We are not a genetic accident. We did not evolve. The Sabbath reminds us that we are not alone on a spinning globe of ash hurling through space at 67,000 miles per hour on a journey to nowhere. The Sabbath is a weekly reminder that we were created by God and that we can rest in His care.

It calls us to enter His heavenly rest. It calls us to experience a foretaste of heaven today. It calls us to a relationship with our Creator that will continue throughout eternity. The Sabbath is in actuality an advance on eternity. There is much more coming, but in the Sabbath we have the first installment. Is it possible that in the busy-ness of life, filled with anxiety and consumed with stress, we have missed one of God's greatest blessings? Is it possible God is calling us to something deeper, something broader, something higher, something larger than we have ever experienced before? Is it possible God longs for us to see a new depth of meaning in the Sabbath? Is it possible God yearns for us to experience genuine peace this Sabbath?

Entering true Sabbath rest is by no means some Old Testament legalistic requirement. Sabbath rest is a symbol of our rest in Christ. We cease trying to create salvation on the basis of our own efforts. God has saved us in Christ.

When Jesus voluntarily poured out His life on the cross, He died the death we deserve. He gave His perfect life as a substitute for our sinful life. The Sabbath is not a symbol of legalism. It is rather an eternal reminder that we rest in Him for our salvation. The Carpenter from Nazareth built a special dwelling for us. We can find refuge there. We can be safe there. His work is complete. It is finished. We can know that in Christ we are accepted by our loving heavenly Father. When we rest on the Sabbath, we are resting in His loving care. We are resting in His righteousness. Sabbath rest is a symbol of a faith experience in Jesus. It is a graphic illustration of our trust in Him.

All week we work, but on the seventh day we rest. We turn from our works to a total rest in Christ. In Jesus we have someplace to belong. We need not stressfully work out our own salvation. Our lives need not be filled with guilt and fear and anxiety. The Sabbath reveals the restful attitude of total dependence on the Christ who created us and redeemed us. Salvation comes only through Jesus. We do not deserve it. We cannot earn it. We rest and receive it by faith.

Here's another reason God gave us the Sabbath. It shows that the Lord is the one who sanctifies us. How is that? Well, that's what God did to the seventh day. It was an ordinary slice of time just like any other at the end of Creation week, but God set this day apart. He sanctified it. And through the Sabbath, God tells us, "That's what I want to do for you, too. I want to set you apart as My special child. I want to pour Myself into you. I want to sanctify you. I want to share My holiness with you."

The Sabbath reminds us of where we develop character—in relationship with our heavenly Father and with Jesus Christ. The Sabbath is a continual living promise of God's ability to help us grow through all the ups and downs, tragedies and triumphs, of our lives. We need that distinctive time with the heavenly Father. We need Sabbath quality time with the God who sanctifies us, the God who helps us keep growing. The Sabbath has continued in the weekly cycle from the dawn of Creation until now. The Sabbath began in the Garden of Eden, and the Sabbath will be celebrated when this earth is renewed after Christ's second coming. It is the very basis of all worship. Writing in the Bible's last book, John states, "You are worthy, O Lord, to receive glory and honor and power; for You created all things, and by Your will they exist and were created" (Revelation 4:11). We exist by the will of God. We are not some random assortment of molecules or some haphazard arrangement of cells. Sabbath worship is a glorious testimony of the love of our Creator God who has given us the gift of life.

The prophet Isaiah talks about a time God will make the "new heavens and the new earth." He says, " 'It shall come to pass that from one New Moon to another, and from one Sabbath to another, all flesh shall come to worship before Me,' says the Lord" (Isaiah 66:22, 23). Every Sabbath in the earth made new we will enter the joy of worship with the entire universe. The Father, Son, and Holy Spirit will lead us in a symphony of praise in New Jerusalem's city of refuge. There we will be secure forever.

The New Jerusalem: The Ultimate City of Refuge

God can encourage us in remarkable ways when we are experiencing trials. The apostle John was exiled on the rocky, barren isle of Patmos off the coast of Greece. Imagine his loneliness. He was separated from his family, friends, and Christian brothers and sisters. Loneliness often leads to discouragement. But John was not alone. Day by day he spent time with Jesus in prayer and meditation. Then one day the glory of God overwhelmed Him. The angel of the Lord descended from heaven and revealed the future in amazing symbols of prophetic imagery. John wrote down the visions the angel gave him so that we can read them today. They are in the Bible's last book, Revelation. These prophetic revelations reveal that God is in control of the destiny of this planet. The book of Revelation climaxes with the Holy City, the New Jerusalem, descending from heaven to earth. Deep within our hearts we long for security. We long for a better world, where heartache and sorrow are over. The New Jerusalem is our final safe haven. It is God's eternal city of refuge. Here in the presence of Jesus we will be eternally secure.

Writing about this city, the apostle John says, "Now I saw a new heaven and a new earth, for the first heaven and the first earth had passed away. Also there was no more sea. Then I, John, saw the holy city, New Jerusalem, coming down out of heaven from God, prepared as a bride adorned for her husband. And I heard a loud voice from heaven saying, 'Behold, the tabernacle of God is with men, and He will dwell with them, and they shall be His people. God Himself will be with them and be their God. And God will wipe away every tear from their eyes; there shall be no more death, nor sorrow, nor crying. There shall be no more pain, for the former things have passed away' " (Revelation 21:1-4). The apostle saw the final act in the great controversy between good and evil. Wickedness, evil, and sin will be finally and fully destroyed. The Holy City, New Jerusalem, will descend from heaven. Planet Earth, which has been so consumed with conflict, strife, war, natural disasters, crime, sickness, and disease, will be made new again. The earth will be created in Edenic splendor. This planet in rebellion will become the center of God's new world. The tabernacle of God, the very dwelling place of God, will reside in the earth made new. God will dwell with His people. Love will reign. Joy will fill our hearts. Disease, disaster, and death will be gone forever.

One day wickedness will give way to righteousness. One day war will surrender to peace. One day sickness will be eradicated, and our bodies will flourish in abundant health. One day evil will be defeated, and goodness will reign. One day poverty will give way to plenty. One day the devil will be finally destroyed, and Jesus will be Lord of all and King of kings. Although evil seems so strong, wickedness so great, and sin so powerful, the faithful and true witness, the resurrected Christ, the ruler over the kings of the earth—the true King of kings—is really, truly coming again, and we will live with Him forever and ever and ever and ever.

One day when George MacDonald, the great Scottish preacher and writer, was talking with his son, the conversation turned to heaven and the prophets' version of the end of all things.

"It seems too good to be true," the son said at one point.

A smile crossed MacDonald's whiskered face. "Nay," he replied. "It is just so good it must be true!" (Philip Yancey, *Disappointment With God*, p. 97). The old preacher was right. No human mind could dream up an ending to the conflict between good and evil that would be so glorious. The joys of heaven are far beyond our comprehension. Our heavenly Father has something prepared for us that will satisfy every need of our hearts. Most of all, we will be content because we will be with Jesus throughout all eternity. He is the source of our joy. He is the wellspring of our happiness. He quenches the thirst of our souls for a deep, lasting love that never ceases. We were made to be loved, and throughout the ceaseless ages of eternity we will experience more and more of His love.

Christ's unconditional, unending, unfathomable love will continually find new ways to bring joy to our hearts and make us happy. We will discover in the world made new that the heavenly Trio, the Father, Son, and Holy Spirit, find Their greatest delight in bringing joy to heaven's inhabitants.

Would you like to experience joy unspeakable, happiness without measure, a peace beyond human understanding, and a divine love that overflows from your heart to those around you? Would you like to have abundant health, boundless energy, and unending vitality? Would you like to develop every talent, explore unnumbered worlds, travel to vast civilizations that have never fallen by sin, and continually discover new mysteries of the universe? Would you like to fellowship with the greatest minds that have ever lived, and develop relationships that are deep and lasting? Heaven is not too good to be true; it is too good not to be true. All of this is for you. Heaven is your home. Why not right now open your heart to the living Christ and surrender your life fully to Him? Accept His love. Receive His forgiveness. Ask Him for the power to live a new life, and rejoice that you are a child of God who one day will be secure in His love forever in the New Jerusalem.

FREE Lessons at www.DiscoverOnline.org.uk

Call:
+44(0)1923 672606

Write:
Adventist Discovery Centre
Stanborough Park
Watford, Hertfordshire
WD25 9JU, UK

It's easy to learn more about the Bible!